WHAT'S UNDER THAT HAT?

DR. LOIS JORDAN

WITH VALERIE CONNELLY

Nightengale Press
©2024 All Rights Reserved

WHAT'S UNDER THAT HAT?

©2024 Dr. Lois Jordan

No part of this book may be reproduced or transmitted in any form or by any means, electronic or mechanical, including photocopying, recording, or by any information storage and retrieval system without written permission from the publisher, except for the inclusion of brief quotations in articles and reviews.

If you purchased this book without a cover, you should be aware that this book is stolen property. It was reported as "unsold and destroyed" to the publisher, and neither the author nor the publisher has received any payment for this "stripped book."

Library of Congress Cataloging-in-Publication Data
Jordan, Dr. Lois,
WHAT'S UNDER THAT HAT?/ Dr. Lois Jordan
ISBN 13: 978-1-945257-48-3
Genre: Memoir

Published in the United States of America
©2024
Nightengale Press
www.nightengalepress.com

10 9 8 7 6 5 4 3 2 1

ACKNOWLEDGMENTS

I am most grateful to Valerie Connelly, who is a book publisher, author, composer, screenwriter and producer. She has gotten me through the strenuous development of this book, *What's Under That Hat? — A Life Story of Perseverance*.

I would also like to thank S. J. Ellis and Dr. Bernadine DePolus for their ideas and their guidance in shaping this book.

I am greatly appreciative to Ashlyn for her support in my gathering materials for publishing this book.

INTRODUCTION

WHAT'S UNDER THAT HAT?

"What lies under that hat?
A string of pearls?
Prayer hands?
Knees scarred from praying?
A mind like a diamond?
The thoughts of an educator?
A heart of gold?
A churchgoers?"

—S. J. Ellis

WHO AM I?

Over the course of my life, I've been called many things: trailblazer, leader, real estate investor, lady, politician, student, and teacher. Poor and rich. Churchgoer. I've lived in the worst neighborhood in Nashville and I've sat on Nashville's City Council, becoming the first elected female of any race ever to do so. I've been both a student and a teacher in government and civics classes in Metropolitan Nashville Public Schools. I've benefited from priceless advice from several distinguished mentors and in turn, dispensed some wisdom of my own. I executed a plan that I had nurtured since I was a little girl. I've spent countless hours in church.

Along the way, I've been lucky enough to win several honors, awards, and certification of appreciation. To name a few, I was named a 2000 Woman of Achievement, a Personality of the South, a Noble American of the Bicentennial Era, a Community Leader of Noteworthy Americans. I was recognized as a woman of distinction by the Professional Organization of Women of Excellence Recognized (P.O.W.E.R.), and I was awarded a certificate for Membership in the Rotary Club of Hendersonville, TN, being the first African-American woman inducted. I earned the Tier of Excellence of the Oxford Who's Who Award. I also received honors for the Nashville Symphony Guild, the March of Dimes, the Friends of Children's Hospital, and Phi Beta Kappa. I served as a board trustee for Volunteer State College and as the chairwoman of the Holidayfest Saint Nicholas Ball. I was recently featured in *Hendersonville Lifestyle Magazine* and *Essence* magazine named me an "Essence Woman" in 1974.

Why am I writing this book? I'm writing for today's youth. I want them to understand they can transcend the circumstances they are born into. I want them to benefit from some of the things I've learned over the years, including the importance of finding mentors and the centrality of Faith. I want them to take an active role in their own education.

I want the youth to understand a message delivered by Dr. Bruce Chesser of the First Baptist Church of Hendersonville, TN delivered during one of his services: *"Never waste a loss. You must learn from that loss."*

I also want them to understand another message that delivered by the Reverend Lester E. Stratton of Rockland Baptist Church:

"Sometimes it hurt, but it didn't hurt me."

I wasn't born with a silver spoon in my mouth. Quite the opposite, actually. I was born in the toughest housing project in Nashville. And that's where my story begins.

DEDICATION

To my churches, to my family to my mentors and to God.

To Harold Nubia, my deceased husband, who was so patient with me throughout this process.

To my nieces, Francis Jones Coleman, Jennifer Jones, and Sondralyn Jordan, and to my beloved brother Cardell Jordan and his wife, Sondra.

I am grateful to Jackie Dooyema, who was my therapist and was also the Director of Results Physiotherapy. Special thanks is extended to Andrea Currey, therapist, along with Kimberly McDonald and Kyla Paz, who welcomed me with open arms to solve some of my medical and physical concerns during the course of my developing my book.

To Dr. Phillip Wines who is a cardiologist who helped my heart keep pumping and who helped me remain calm instead of stressed out. And also, thank to his medical assistant, Nancy Smith.

I am sincerely grateful to Bonnie Edwards, who was there for me to enjoy the symphony, ballet and opera during the course of my telling my story.

WHAT'S UNDER THAT HAT?

CHAPTER 1

LOSS IS LIFE'S TEACHER

As Lois walks toward the room where her husband lies waiting for the end, she barely sees anything in the crowded hallway, until she nears his room. Then she sees only the room numbers, 210, 212, 214. Then she arrives at 216. She stops and stares at the number.

"Yes, that's right."

She slowly opens the door and tiptoes toward the only chair in the room, on the window side of his bed.

"I'm here, Harold," she whispers.

He doesn't respond. Lois sits motionless in the private hospital room chair. The quiet beeping of the machines connected to her husband to keep him comfortable sound like intruders in their last moments together. Harold Nubia stirs briefly but never opens his eyes.

"Lois?"

"Yes, my dear. I'm right here."

"I don't want to die."

"Hold on. I don't want you to die either."

"I want to get better."

"I guess the doctors will do what they can for you. Hold on, Boo, you know I love you. I'll be here for you until the very end."

WHAT'S UNDER THAT HAT?

Starting on the first night, Lois talks to Harold as though she knows he hears every word. She cries while she's there, too, but she doesn't want him to know she is emotional. She knows his time is coming soon, but she doesn't feel she can prepare for it. So, she comes to see him three days and nights in a row. The time she spends with him is exhausting. The fourth night, October 9th 2022, she stays home and sleeps in her own bed.

At 11pm a disturbance outside wakes her. She looks out the window and sees police cars. She calls her neighbor.

"What are all these police cars doing out here?"

"They're looking for you."

"For me? For what?"

The doorbell rings and the two police officers are standing there like they aren't sure what to say.

"Are you Dr. Lois Jordan?"

"Why?"

"We're here to let you know Harold has passed away."

She opens the door wide and begins to scream and holler.

"Oh, no! Oh, no! I promised him I'd stay with him until the very end. He can't be gone, not yet!"

Another man, a spiritual counselor, who arrives as Lois is shouting, takes her into the house to console her.

"Lois, who is your minister?" asks the younger policeman.

"Dr. Bruce Chester at First Baptist Church," says Lois, as she goes to the desk, fumbles with the address book, and brings it back to the policeman. "Here is his number." She gives the address book to the policeman, who steps out of the room to make the call.

Dr. Chester arrives at Lois's door only minutes after that.

"Lois, I'm here to help you pray for Harold. We'll make plans for his funeral in a day or two. Come sit down with me here."

WHAT'S UNDER THAT HAT?

He leads her to a chair in her living room. The spiritual counselor and the two policemen join Lois and Dr. Chester. Prayers and encouragement fill the room for more than an hour.

When Lois finally settles down and is no longer crying, the policemen realize they can let leave her alone to grieve.

"We're so sorry for your loss. If you need anything, let us know," they say as they go to the front door.

"Thank you for coming." The words feel strange on her lips.

Then the spiritual counselor and the minister stand to leave.

"You're going to be all right," Dr. Bruce Chester says as he hugs Lois.

"Thank you all for coming to me tonight. It helps—I feel blessed that you all came to tell me of Harold's passing. I'm sure your words and guidance will stay with me long after tonight."

But, when the door swings closed, Lois knows she is alone to face the future on her own.

She goes up to her bedroom and lies down. Sleep is elusive. Her memories of Harold come into her thoughts. When she closes her eyes, she sees his face floating before her. He's smiling. That allows her to drift into a fitful slumber.

CHAPTER 2

BEGINNINGS & MENTORS

"Surround yourself only with people who are going to take you higher."
—*Oprah Winfrey*

Life in the J. C. Napier Projects, in Nashville, Tennessee was hard. The Napier housing project stood among the worst—and all that term implies—for how urban, low-income housing projects were conceived to be. The current-day website, Napier Voices describes this housing facility, in part, like this:

Built in 1939, by the Nashville Housing Authority, J.C Napier and Boscobel Heights, now known as James A. Cayce, were two options that people from low- income families could offer to stay at in a time when the cost of living was rising. Systematically the people that started to settle within these two public housing communities were predominantly African American. With little resources, lack of transportation, and the need to provide left many people with no other choice but to live in these two housing projects.

The demographics that is represented within the Napier community is one that flourishes within a desolate valley, desolate because it lies close to the downtown area of Nashville, labeled as being in a food desert, and surrounded by a wide spectrum of warehouses and industrial area.

WHAT'S UNDER THAT HAT?

The J. C. Napier Project consists of 861 subsidized units with roughly 16,000 residents, with a median income of $18,000 per household.

To this day Napier is categorized as a high crime area where prostitution, drugs, and joblessness exists. The media is prudent in always igniting the ideology that the area is neither safe nor a pleasant place. But if this idea is conceptualized and the heart of Napier is analyzed, it is a valley of diversity and people that know and understand their situation, but likewise still hold on tight to hope and happiness.

Lois describes the residents as close and very friendly. Everyone knew everyone else. And in many ways, they all took care of each other.

"The houses are of dark red brick construction, with clothes hanging on the line, children hanging out the windows or running from one to another's houses. The yards are green with cut grass, the sidewalks to the apartments are narrow, but even so, walking is easy. There are trees scattered around the yards, where children often climbed and played in them. The houses are two stories high with a peaked roof, and the bedrooms are upstairs, and downstairs you have the kitchen and the living room. The windows are double hung, with screens that also could be pushed up.

The Napier homes consume several city blocks, facing shops, stores and small businesses where residents could shop conveniently, and so they did. The neighborhood is friendly and familiar, sometimes to the level of being nosy.

If you live at the beginning of the projects, you'd hear the sounds of the city, trucks, cars, ambulances, sirens. However, in the interior grid of the projects the city sounds become muffled, and you hear the voices of your neighbors. Punctuating these normal sounds of living, gun shots would sometimes ring out. Some people would run inside, fearful of the violence. Others would be curious and try to find out where the shots were coming from.

The floors are concrete, walls are sheet rock, and the coal bin on the back porch is filled at the beginning of winter and lasts until Spring. The cooking stove is electric, and the electricity works, and the water always flows.

All the floor plans of the houses are the same, but each family has its own personality decorating the house."

CAMILLA EDDINGS JORDAN

My mother kept the house meticulously clean. Shiny maroon paint on the floors, clean kitchen with no dishes left around. When it was my turn to wash dishes, I paid my three sisters fifteen cents to wash and ten cents to dry them so I wouldn't have to do that work. They were happy to get the money for washing dishes. As a teenager, I earned this money baby-sitting. And when I had to do it, I'd hide dishes in the oven. If my mother found out, I'd get a switch spanking, and I still had to wash the dishes with food dried on so that it was harder to clean.

All the walls were painted white and housed pictures of landscapes and nature themes. In the living room, there was antique furniture which my mother and grandmother both loved. My mother, Camilla, and her mother, Alice—who was mixed race, half white and half black—both walked tall and strong. They both knew their minds.

The bedroom I shared with my sisters contained twin beds. I used to hide under my bed with blankets around me to have my solitude or to see what my sisters would do thinking I wasn't there. I saved money in a little piggy bank. My sisters took money from my piggy bank by shaking it out.

WHAT'S UNDER THAT HAT?

Camilla was an avid tennis player and would go out to play most of the day. I loved to watch her play when the opportunity arose. My dad, John Henry Jordan, a sophisticated man, used the bathroom as his parlor to read and meditate. I followed in his footsteps and to this day I have magazines, books and notepads in the bathroom.

I was always inquisitive. One day I heard my daddy talking to his girlfriend on the phone. When he came downstairs with a pillowcase full of clothes, I asked him, "Where you going, Daddy?"

"To the laundry and I'll see you all later on." But he never came back. I told my mother, "Mama, Daddy's gone! What are we going to do?"

Camilla called a welfare worker, Miss Taylor, to come to the house. She came and saw that it was clean and beautiful.

"Camilla, why not sell your antiques to get some money to live on?"

"You know, Miss Taylor, you can just walk out that door and let it hit you on the backside, because you'll do better by leaving than you did when you came in here," Camilla said. And Miss Taylor did leave the house. Camilla then called us all together.

"Listen to me now, girls. Your daddy isn't coming back. So, I'll get a job and work to support us. I'll be gone to work, and I don't ask anyone for anything. If you get too hungry before I get home, put your head in the sugar bowl, so you can wait till I get home."

My sisters and I did 'put our heads in the sugar bowl' when our mother was late. I learned independence and toughness from my mother's example. You don't go to others for help. You help yourself. And if you can't help yourself—you do without.

My sister, Henerine was a couple of years younger than I was. She grew up, married, and had two boys. One is now deceased and the other, Marvel, takes care of his mother because she has dementia.

WHAT'S UNDER THAT HAT?

Madeline was a couple of years younger than Henerine. She lived in Hawaii for twenty-five years and now she's in Nashville. She can do the hula.

Brenda was a couple of years younger than Madeline, but she died of lung cancer several years ago.

Harriet was a couple of years younger than Brenda, and she still lives in Hendersonville. She has two daughters.

When we were children, we pestered our mother about not having a brother.

"Mama, we want a *brooother*! Mama we want a brooother!" we said over and over again. Then one day, Camilla said, "Well, I'll go get you one!" And she did. But we never knew Cardell's father. Cardell was the only brother and the youngest child, but he had a different father and so was very much younger than his five sisters. Cardell thought his father was our father, but Camilla was never truthful about it, and she likely didn't tell him anything. She was very secretive in order to protect us all.

Cardell and his wife, Sandra, live in St. Louis. The had two boys and one girl. He is an artist and a photographer. He was a member of the Army for more than twenty years, and he takes care of his big sister—me.

I took all of this in stride because it was just family life.

When I was in Middle School and High School, I wanted to get mother and father to live together again, just so my friends could stay the night for sleepovers. But because we didn't have both our parents in the home, our friends couldn't come spend the night. Their parents prevented them coming to stay at a sleepover at our house.

Years later, Camilla went to Chicago to see if John Henry would come home. It didn't turn out the way I wanted it to. My mother said, "He's still wearing the same shoes he had on when he left."

WHAT'S UNDER THAT HAT?

And one time I went to Chicago and went to his office to surprise him. I scared him half to death! He was all choked up to see me. I stuck around a while to be nosy and to be in the way. When I left it was after a friendly conversation. I never saw him again, although I did call John Henry when I finished college. He was very excited that I had graduated.

John Doe was my first love. (Of course, that's not his real name.) He was from an affluent family. They knew me and seemed to like me a lot, but John Doe and I weren't meant to be. He wasn't true to me. At one point he made another girl pregnant, and she knew about me, so, we didn't date anymore. I insisted that he marry her and I got them to go to the church. Then, after a baby was born, John Doe had to go to work, and he didn't have anyone to keep the child because his wife had left him. He called me and I went over to babysit, but only once or twice because I was scared to death, not knowing what might happen.

I loved my grandmother, Alice—also known as Big Mama—because my younger sisters—in particular Brenda—meddled in my things and wore my clothes. As a result, I left home and went to stay with Alice. Here's what happened that made me leave home. Remember, this was the last episode in a long string of episodes that became impossible to put up with anymore.

My four sisters and I shared a room with two beds that divided the space. Brenda had her things and I had mine. One day, my favorite sweater, black with buttons down the front, had come back from the dry cleaners in a bag. I left it there for a while, not having a reason wear it. The day I decided to wear it, I noticed the bag was already open.

"Oh, Brenda, what have you done?" I muttered.

I took the sweater from the bag and found the remnants of

deodorant under the arms. I heard myself shouting and realized I was stomping my feet in anger. I ran through the house looking for Brenda and discovered she was gone.

I went to my mother screaming and hollering, "Brenda got into my things again! I'm sick and tired of this!"

"You both gotta stop messing with each other," Mama said. But I knew she wasn't going to do anything to help me.

"Mama, I'm going to go live with Big Mama. I just can't stand this anymore!"

BIG MAMA — ALICE EDDINGS

I ran up to my room, took my sweater, my clothes, and shoes and put them in a pillowcase. I took the pillowcase off Brenda's pillow and put all my other treasures—my piggy bank, my costume jewelry, and special things I'd collected—into it. Last of all were my books. I'd read them many times, but I loved them, so into the pillowcase they went.

I left the house and headed straight toward Big Mama's house. Her house had a long porch where we often sat and talked. As I walked up the steps to that front porch, I stood a moment outside the door. I let myself feel the emotions of leaving home and the joy of arriving at my grandmother's welcoming arms. I knocked for a little while, and then the door opened and there was my grandmother, Big Mama. She could see I was upset.

"Lois? What in the world happened? Why are you here?"

Tears ran down my face as I explained myself. She wrapped me up in her arms, consoling me, and told me, "Everything's going to be all right. C'mon in."

As time passed, I saw both my mother and my grandmother as my first mentors. But they were such different women.

WHAT'S UNDER THAT HAT?

My mother made it clear that if I wanted something, I had work for it. When my father left, she sat us kids down and spoke to us about how life would change. As we came into the kitchen, we knew something was different.

"Lois, Henerine, Madeline, Brenda, and Harriet. You know your father is gone. I am going to work. We are not taking welfare. We will make our own way. But this is going to affect you, too. Because you must not get in trouble. You will have to work hard at school, and if you want something, you'll have to work for it. I will keep us together, but you have to help."

Harriet, the youngest, looked at her mother with tears in her eyes. "Isn't Daddy coming back?"

All eyes turned toward her, and she knew the answer. From that day forward, we all set about becoming independent and strong.

When I went to live with Big Mama, it took me a while to adjust. Now and then we'd sit in her bedroom. I rocked in the rocking chair, and in the winter, the fireplace kept us warm as we talked about just about everything. But the porch was our most common ground. Big Mama always started the conversation.

"Who do you want to be when you grow up?" she always asked. Then she sat silent waiting for my answer, smiling at me with that supportive expression I came to love.

"I want to be somewhat like you. And I want to go to college to get a good education, so I can do something to help the community serve everyone who lives in the district. You know I love learning about government and history. Economics and finance are essential to understanding how a government works. So, I want to learn about all those disciplines too."

"Oh, that's excellent! I believe you will become known for doing something for the greater good. I'm so proud of you for aspiring to greater things."

And from that day on, I knew I would keep that promise. I earned a real estate license, sold houses, and saved my money. I bought and renovated thirteen houses and sold them to people who loved them.

After one of Big Mama's delicious meals, she and I often sat on the porch just chat-chattin'. This is where I learned about her life.

Big Mama's real name was Alice Eddings. She came from a rural Tennessee life where she worked for a family keeping the house and living almost as a member of the family. When she was old enough, they suggested she marry a man they knew, and she did not object. So, she married Walter Eddings in a small, country, traditional wedding where they did a ceremony where the bride and the groom jump the broom.

"Jumping the broom not only symbolizes the sweeping away of evil, past loves and the old you, but it also represents jumping into a new life together and setting up your household." (https://www.theknot.com/content/jumping-the-broom)

The history of jumping the broom is both fraught and disputed. Some say it dates back to Wales in the 1700s, when the Roman community practiced broomstick weddings since they weren't allowed to wed in Welsh churches. Another theory is that the practice originated in West Africa as a means of cleansing the marriage ceremony from evil spirits while also representing the couple's commitment to each other. While it's unclear which region first began the practice, America's sordid history with the transatlantic slave trade led to the practice making its way to the American South. At this time, many enslaved people practiced broom-jumping to symbolize their union since they weren't afforded civil rights and legally recognized weddings.

Today, the practice continues at many African American weddings by Black couples as a way of paying tribute to the struggles of their forebearers while also celebrating Black Love and reclaiming ownership of the ritual that was first brought into existence by those seeking freedom from oppression."

At some point Alice and Walter moved to Nashville and made a family of six children, two boys and four girls.

And my grandmother taught me exactly how to act. She was a lady. I followed in her footsteps and wanted to be elegant, sophisticated, and ladylike just as she was.

Many years later, as Alice lay on her deathbed the phone kept ringing and no one came to answer it. I walked toward her room saying, "Big Mama, Big Mama, why don't you answer the phone? My goodness!" As I entered her room, I saw she was dead. And it just tore me up.

I screamed and cried. I called my mother, and she called my sisters, and everyone came when they could.

The Holmes Funeral Home came and took Big Mama to their facility and the funeral was a few days later. The service was held at the funeral home. Family, friends of Big Mama, and friends of the family came and filled the room till there was no more standing room.

✿

It's true that my first mentors in life were my mother and Big Mama. But following alongside were several others who helped me define my path in life.

WHAT'S UNDER THAT HAT?
ELIZABETH REED

Elizabeth Reed was a hands-on, experienced Civics teacher. She didn't just read the book. She took the students into the lesson. Role playing was a consistent part of that process.

"Class, starting today we're going to learn what it's like to run an election. This will guide you in the future because voting in elections is the basis of our representative democracy. First, you'll decide what two ideas the students will be voting for. Then you'll give speeches and rallies to involve the students. Then you'll hold an election. Whoever gets the most votes wins the election."

I raise my hand. Mrs. Reed calls on me.

"I think the school should have a swimming pool. I'd like to run for election to get a swimming pool for our school."

"Now, remember, we're just role playing, but Lois has a good idea. Do the rest of you want to use her idea? Raise your hand if you agree." All the students raise their hands.

"Now, what is another idea that another of you will promote?"

Henry raises his hand. "I think the school should have new uniforms for the sports teams."

"All right, Class. Raise your hand if you think the school should have new uniforms for the sports teams as the second proposition." All hands went up.

"Good. So now you will count off by 1 and by 2 until the two opposing groups are formed. Lois will be the candidate for getting a swimming pool, and Henry will be the candidate for buying new uniforms for the sports teams. Each team will prepare a speech about why their idea should win the vote, and each team will also plan a ten-minute-long rally to get their idea to the students. You have the rest of this class to plan, and tomorrow we'll write the speeches, and the next day we'll design the rallies, and the final day, we will actually present the speeches at the two rallies. One of the other Civics classes will join us, and we'll hold the elections right after the rallies. Everyone is to contribute to the project. I'll be available to answer questions."

Mrs. Reed often took her students to the city hall to see the government at work. They watched Council meetings and met with Council Members.

The result is, years later, when I became a teacher of government studies, I had voting machines brought in. And we discussed certain issues the students wanted to debate before getting to vote. I brought leaders from the community to come into the classroom to speak with the students and issues of the day. I brought Don Sunquest, Governor, and the Ambassador to France, Joe. M. Rodgers. I included Payton Manning in my list, along with Winfield Dunn, Governor.

ೞಚ

After graduating, I kept in close contact with Elizabeth Reed. She visited me at home fairly often because it was a good way for her to get out of the house, and because she wanted to know how I was doing with meetings in the community. I always served tea and something to eat when Mrs. Reed came to visit.

ೞಚ   TEATIME ೞಚ

Lois stands at the kitchen counter, putting together the little finger sandwiches she always serves when Elizabeth Reed comes to visit. The teapot whistles and Lois turns off the stove. She pours the hot water into the porcelain teapot where the leaves will steep until teatime. She places some home-baked sugar cookies next to the finger-sandwiches on one of her favorite antique plates painted with pink and blue flowers and green leaves.

The doorbell plays its tune.

"Oh my! She's a little bit early," Lois whispers under her breath as she walks into the living room to open the front door.

"Hello, Lois. It's so lovely to be here," Mrs. Reed says as the door opens.

Lois opens the screen door, and her mentor enters the room.

"It's so good to see you again, Mrs. Reed, please come sit while I get the tea."

Mrs. Reed walks to the couch and sits on the first of the three cushions where she always sits to visit. Lois quickly returns from the kitchen with the teapot and the plate of finger sandwiches and sugar cookies. She sets the teapot on the trivet next to the two teacups and saucers, plates and napkins on the low table in front of the couch. Lois offers Ms. Reed the plate and she takes a finger sandwich and a cookie.

"Thank you, dear. You baked these cookies yourself?"

"I did. Just for you."

Mrs. Reed takes a bite of the cookie. "Always so delicious!"

Both women smile with shared understanding. Lois then pours the hot tea into the teacups and sets one in front of Mrs. Reed. Lois sits at the other end of the couch.

Mrs. Reed asks, "How are things going with the meetings you're planning for the community?"

"Well, you know," Lois says finishing a bite of finger sandwich, "there are so many details to complete to make sure everyone comes to the meetings. I have been working with one of the ministers in the Seay Hubbard Methodist Church to set up a regular schedule of events. I think that will be better than going to several different places in rotation. If it's a regular meeting place, more people will come because there's less confusion about where to go."

"You know, Lois, I am proud of you for listening to me in my classes back in the day. You've done me a great honor by becoming an educator."

"You mentored me all along the way, and for that I can't ever repay you. Thank you, Mrs. Reed."

"You're welcome, dear. You make me happy. And I'm glad we share teatime every now and then. So, thank you for brightening up my retirement."

Three more interesting little facts about Mrs. Reed. Her husband was the first Black writer for the Nashville Tennessean, she wrote the school song and her son married Sarah Vaughn, the world-renowned singer.

ଓଓଓଃ

MRS. GALLOWAY

Mrs. Galloway gave me the confidence to dress the part to show others where I was headed. And I learned to make a lasting impression on just about everybody I met.

Mrs. Galloway inducted me into the sorority she was in. When I went to Washington D.C., she taught me table manners and how to use all the silverware. I didn't know what the little bowl with warm water was all about—to rinse your fingers before dinner.

I had a tailor who designed my clothes for me, Miss Lucy, and I still wear some of the suits she made to this day. I was noted for wearing suits, hats and gloves and pearls. And I still do. Fabric red, black, beige, silk, light-weight wool, gabardine, knits, and jersey.

WHAT'S UNDER THAT HAT?

MR. WILLIAM JONES

Throughout my schooling, there was another teacher who was always looking out for me. His name was Mr. William Jones and he was a math teacher. He and his wife, Ann looked out for me and showed me a great deal of love during some difficult years. Mr. Jones figured out at some point that I wasn't getting everything I needed at home.

Thanks to the many small kindnesses of Mr. and Mrs. Jones, I never had to worry about having something to eat at school. They made sure I got a hot lunch like everyone else, instead of having to take a brown bag. When everybody else had a plate, so did I, and that made things comfortable for me at school in the lunchroom. From elementary grades through high school Mr. Jones paid the schools for my cafeteria lunches, and I am forever grateful for his generosity.

ROBERT EMMITT LILLARD

In 1932, while Robert Emmitt Lillard was working as a city garage attendant, he entered Nashville's Kent College of Law. He attended law classes five nights a week, began working for Nashville's Fire Engine Company No.11, all the while studying to earn his legal education, He graduated in 1935, passing the bar a year later.

In 1951 he received a disability pension from the fire department. He then entered the predominantly black Third District,

Second Ward city councilman race. Even though his opponent, the incumbent Charles Castleman, had the support of the Democratic Mayor Thomas Cummings, and even though white politicians offered Lillard money and jobs to drop out of the race, he announced he could not be bought out or frightened out, and that the white politicians would have to beat him out. In May, Lillard won the runoff election and became the first Afro-American elected to the Nashville City Council.

Robert Lillard went on to serve on the city council for twenty years, and never missed a regular meeting. Meanwhile, his political activism and law practice did well. He was admitted to the federal district court in 1955, the US. Court of Appeals, the Sixth Circuit court in 1957, and the U.S. Supreme Court in 1962.

Lillard established the Tennessee Federation of Democratic Leagues and campaigned for JFK in 1960. He turned down an offer to become Nashville's assistant U.S. Attorney. Yet, in 1964 and 1967 Lillard was appointed to the Tennessee Board of Pardons and Paroles by two Democratic governors. Governor Ray Blanton appointed Lillard as judge to the First Circuit Court, Tenth Judicial District. At the end of August 1978, Lillard retired from the bench. He passed away thirteen years later in 1991 and was buried in Nashville's Greenwood Cemetery.

༄༅

Attorney Robert Lillard was a member of the City Council just before I took his seat when he retired from politics in 1974.

One day, Mr. Lillard called me into his office.

"Lois, I have some things I'd like to say before I retire. We've worked together on many community matters. And you've seen how I work."

"Yes, Sir, I have. You've taught me how to go with the flow or against it to manage the chaos of political discourse. I learned from you how to read between the lines of what people say and what they actually mean."

"Those are useful skills. But I think of you as an ambitious professional who I can help rise to the mountaintop. However, I can only assist you from time to time. The real work is up to you."

ಬಿಂಡ

And guide me he did, all along my political journey. I knew he was actively helping me, but I ignored it. I stood firm in my own belief in myself, and he taught me how to use that belief to progress upward in the political scene.

Robert Lillard gave me the self-confidence to express myself and go after what I wanted to accomplish in life. I learned from him how to bring prestigious people into the community as I was trying to uplift people and make them aware of what was going on in the city of Nashville. Urban renewal, repairing streets, new housing developments, economic zones to attract business, trying to maintain a good relationship with the police to deal with crime.

Many times, knowledgeable people in governmental institutions (chief of police, overseers of housing development, mayors, State legislators) were invited to come talk with community leaders about the development of the city and how it would affect them and the residents in their communities.

I made contacts with the leadership. I came up with ideas and passed them by Robert Lillard, who, as a prominent lawyer was able to introduce me to the Who's Who of people best suited to inform the community members.

I worked with Robert Lillard who guided me to meet with the leaders and become familiar with them and I got to know them personally, so they were able to work with me on the different projects important to the communities at the time.

Over the years, Robert Lillard gave me the courage and the means to deliver my thoughts and beliefs in a convincing manner when talking with leaders, and the man on the street and to not take "no" for an answer. There is often a compromise or a way to make something happen that could advance the growth of the community, except for the people standing in the way who wanted to keep the status quo. Lillard gave me the confidence to convince others to change their point of view. And that gave me great confidence in myself. As an example, there were no cooling services in the projects. I was instrumental in getting the buildings retrofitted with fans and air-conditioning, which was good for the health of the people who lived there.

CHAPTER 3

GIRL FRIENDS & BOY FRIENDS

AUDREY BRYANT

I remember Audrey as a mystical person, who could see the real person in others. In high school, we became very good friends, and I eventually went to live with her family.

All through high school Audrey performed on television as a singer and pantomimist. Sometimes when she was invited to sing at events, she would ask me to dance creative modern dance as she sang. The audiences enjoyed our performances because they were so different.

Audrey's mother, Ellen, always dressed for the occasion. Whether playing golf or attending an exclusive social event, she stood out from the crowd. She saw to it that I was well dressed and well groomed, too, just as she did for Audrey. She bought clothes both for Audrey and for me, which made me feel cared for. Her kindness let me know that Ellen saw me as a welcome member of her family.

The Bryant family lived in a ranch-style house, where Audrey, her parents and I all had separate bedrooms. I loved having my own space when I wanted some privacy.

WHAT'S UNDER THAT HAT?

I recall that every morning before school, the routine was the same.

☙❧

The quiet of the house breaks at dawn with the sound of Baby Ben alarm clocks. Audrey rolls over to stop the loud clanging of the ringer and then turns over to try to sleep a few minutes more. I wake with a start and quickly silence the intruder's clanging voice. I get right up and go into the bathroom. A few minutes later, Audrey comes in laughing.

"What's so funny?" I ask.

"I don't know. I guess I think I'm silly for trying to go back to sleep," Audrey replies.

"Well, once the day begins it's hard to return to dreaming. Might as well just get up," I say through a mouthful of toothpaste.

Ellen knocks on the door. "I'm heading to the kitchen to make breakfast. Please don't dawdle. You know 7a.m. comes fast around here," she says back over her shoulder as she walks down the hallway toward the kitchen.

We girls run to our rooms to dress.

"I'll see you at the table!" Audrey says loud enough for the walls to crack.

"I'll get there before you do!" I shout back.

Then we race into the dining room to gather up our books and papers from the study session the night before. We waltz into the kitchen.

On the kitchen table two plates of eggs and bacon, two bowls with cereal and a pitcher of milk stand ready for the onslaught. Audrey and I begin to eat as if the food will evaporate from the plate before we can finish. The orange juice washes down the grape-jelly-slathered toast just as the bus honks outside.

WHAT'S UNDER THAT HAT?

"C'mon! We're going to miss the bus!" I say, grabbing my books and running out the door. Audrey follows close behind and jumps into the bus behind me. The door slams shut behind her. Ellen waves at us as the bus drives away.

The seats are nearly full of laughing, chattering teen-agers, all talking at once. I slide into the window seat of one of the benches, and Audrey sets beside me.

"I don't know how we manage to do this every day without missing the bus," Audrey says, laughing and catching her breath.

"I'm sure glad we always make it! It's a long walk to the school from here."

The bus driver revs the engine and the gears groan in protest as he pushes the bus into first gear. Then second. Then third. And then, the bus rolls to a stop at the next corner to pick up more teen-agers to fill the last spots in the bus.

"All right y'all! Sit down so we can get movin'!" the driver shouts over the din. He throws the bus into gear and drives down the street. Ellen watches until the bus rounds the curve and drives out of sight.

Audrey and I ride the noisy bus for about forty minutes. The sound is a happy kind of noise, that laughter and chatter of kids that happens when they think no one is listening.

Finally, the driver pulls up in front of the high school, opens the creaking folding door, and the students jostle each other as they hurry to get off the bus. Some run toward the entrance, while others walk quickly so as to be on time.

As Audrey and I enter the school, we part ways to go to our lockers.

"See you in band later on!" Audrey says as she turns down a different hall where her locker waits for her.

"See you!" I say as I approach my locker. As I turn the combination dial, one of my other girlfriends, Frankie Keeling—also known as Baybay—approaches me, talking loudly and moving quickly through the crowded hall.

"Good morning, Lois. Let's walk together to Algebra class, okay?" Baybay says, cutting through the oncoming students.

"Good morning yourself!" I say. "Sure, just let me get my things together." The locked door wouldn't budge. "Oh, my goodness! What's with my locker today?" She glances at Baybay, who is tapping her foot.

"Come on, girl! Try that combo again. You'll get it right this time."

I make a face at Baybay and then work the series of numbers again. The door pops open and I laugh. "Okay, Algebra, Biology and Civics. That's my morning."

"Let's go! We're going to be late," Baybay says louder, as if I can't hear her every word.

I slam the locker shut, turn the dial to clear the combination, and head into the swarm of students with BayBay chattering to everyone she knows.

Mr. Jones greets his students at the door, handing out a sheet of information about the day's math lesson. As a math teacher, Mr. Jones inspires his students to learn the complicated aspects of Algebra in a clear and logical step-by-step series of smaller lessons that add up to the whole algebraic concept by the end of the year. He is a popular teacher even though he is soft-spoken and serious by nature.

"Good morning, Miss Keeling. Here's your paper."

"Thanks, Mr. Jones," Frankie says scanning the equations on the sheet. "This looks like a tricky turn of the road in Algebra to me."

"It's not as tricky as it looks, you'll see," Mr. Jones replies, handing another paper to me.

"Thanks, Mr. Jones. Please say hello to your wife for me," I whisper as I take the paper from him.

Mr. Jones nods at me and smiles with a knowing smile. I understand he's referencing that he and his wife Ann look out for me. They make sure I get a hot lunch instead of having to take a brown bag. From the beginning of the elementary grades through middle school and now while I'm in high school, they have been paying the school for my cafeteria lunches. Then I go to my desk and settle in for my first class of the morning.

꽃⚭

When the bell rings after English class, I hurry to my locker to put my morning's books away and take the books I'll need for my afternoon classes. And then I make my way through the river of students into the cafeteria for lunch. I carry my punch card in my purse, and juggling my books, I fish the punch card out and hand it to the attendant. Then I take a tray, some silverware and a couple of napkins and move into the food line.

"Spaghetti with meat sauce, apple slices, carrot sticks, and bread and butter are on the menu today," the cook behind the serving table shouts like a circus barker trying to attract people into the main tent. "Get your milk and cookies on the side counter as you leave the line."

I take my plate of spaghetti, the small bowl of apple slices, and a small plate with carrot sticks and bread and butter and arrange them on my tray. Then I walk toward the table where I sit with Audrey and the other girls every day.

"Hey, Lois! Come on, sit next to me," Audrey says, scooching to the left so I can slip into place on the end of the bench. I slide my tray over and sit down. The gossipy-chatter chat is flowing on high speed as I takes a swig of the milk through the straw, and then settle

WHAT'S UNDER THAT HAT?

in to eat the spaghetti first.

"Can you believe it?" Audrey says. "Ben Williams broke up with Maryellen Graves!"

"But they've been going steady for two years! What happened?" I ask, gulping down a mouthful of food.

"Well, the rumor is she was stepping out on him, and he got mad, and just broke it off. He took back his school ring and everything!" BayBay interrupts. "I don't know if she actually did step out on him, but she didn't try to stop him from breaking up!"

"And, that usually means there's someone else in the picture," Audrey adds.

Frankie interjects, "But, who? Ben's on the football team and the basketball team. He's Captain of the Swim team. Who could possibly be a better steady guy than that?"

The loud clanging of the lunchroom bell breaks the conversation. As if one body, all the students stand up, take their trays to the trash bins and dump the leftovers if there are any, and then crowd around the racks where they stack the trays. Then bumping into each other and trying not to drop their books they make their way into the halls for their next classes.

The afternoon passes fast for me in my Civics class, American History and gym classes. Band practice is the last class of the day, and soon Audrey and I are back on the bus heading home.

The moment we enter the house, we smell the delicious aromas of the evening meal. Audrey's mother, Ellen, is busy in the kitchen preparing fried chicken, collard greens, and as the girls push open the swinging door between the kitchen and the dining room, Ellen stands up straight as she takes two loaves of bread from the oven and sets them on racks on the counter to cool.

"Back so soon?" she asks. "Where does the day go?"

WHAT'S UNDER THAT HAT?

Audrey says, "We had a good day, but there's a sizeable stack of homework to do for both of us."

I chime in, "And I have a Civics project to plan for tomorrow's class."

"When is dinner going to be ready?" Audrey smiles at her mother as she slices a couple of pieces of bread from a loaf and puts them on two plates.

"Get some butter and jam, Audrey. And Lois, you get some glasses for milk and knives to spread the butter and jam. I'll bet you're both are ready for a snack before starting that mountain of homework."

Both girls jump into action and in less than a minute they're enjoying the best greeting a mother can give a child after a day at school—bread fresh from the oven with butter and jam, and milk to finish the treat.

About an hour later, both of us are busy concentrating on our studies at the dining room table. Audrey's father, Walter, comes in the door, sets down the newspaper and comes over to us.

"Working on your homework?" he asks.

We both nod but keep working.

"Lois, what are you learning about?"

"I'm just finishing up my Algebra homework, and then I'll be starting to plan a project for Civics. We have two chapters to read in American History—we're studying the American Revolution, and I have to write a poem for English class and study the spelling words."

"And you, Audrey?"

"Ditto, Dad. I have all the same stuff as Lois, just with different teachers. Whew! It's a lot tonight!"

"Well, I know you'll both manage to figure it all out. But dinner's almost ready, so maybe you should move your books and papers

WHAT'S UNDER THAT HAT?

over to the sideboard and set the table."

And with that, Walter goes into the kitchen to see what's for dinner.

After dinner, and after the we finish our homework, Walter gathers the family together.

"I have a surprise to show you. Let's step outside for a minute."

He turns on the outside lights and opens the front door. Everyone walks into the front yard, and there on the driveway is a brand new, baby-blue Cadillac with whitewall tires and so shiny it sparkles in the light.

"Oh, Daddy! What a beautiful car! You buy a new one every year that's more beautiful than the last one!" Audrey gushes.

I stare in amazement and Ellen kisses her husband in delight.

"So, that's my big news. Now let's go watch Ed Sullivan, what you do all say?

"Yes!"

Then the family gathers in the living room to watch television. We enjoy the Ed Sullivan show, laughing at the comedians and a magician whose magic tricks defy explanation. When the show is over, we girls start for the stairs.

"G'night!" we say in unison.

"G'night. Sleep tight!" Ellen and Walter say also in unison.

After high school, I went to college and Audrey did too, but she didn't finish. Over time, our relationship changed, and we grew apart because Audrey sang in clubs, and I was busy organizing communities.

☙❧

WHAT'S UNDER THAT HAT?

FRANKIE KEELING (BAYBAY)

She talked loud and was always moving—fidgety, getting her point over, which she always did. Frankie used a "take charge" tone when she spoke. She did not live in the projects. Later she married a well-respected person in the community who had humble beginnings, but in my opinion he rose to the mountain top. He was one of my mama's favorites. He was an athletic, fit person.

PEGGY HARDING

She talked real soft and lived in a narrow shotgun house. She was an adopted child, adopted by one of the family members. She went to Fisk and became highly educated, and her mannerisms showed that intellect. She played tennis. I hit balls—ran after balls and she played the game. She moved up north and she wanted me to go, but my roots were in Nashville and I wasn't about to leave all the things I was involved in. But we kept in touch until she passed away from Alzheimer's.

BOBBY HEBB

Bobby and I were very good high school friends. Born in Nashville, he was very close to some of the Country and Western Singers. His parents were blind. Bobby was very aggressive and he was a musician. We'd sit on the back porch and talk. "Sunny" was one of his songs. He also played the spoons and tap danced. He asked me to marry him in Pig Latin, and I didn't know what he was saying. He returned to Nashville and later passed away.

WHAT'S UNDER THAT HAT?

JAMES GARRETT

I knew him from elementary school. He was—aggressive and smart. He's till living in Nashville. He has a doctoral degree. At Maharry Medical Hospital, he works in the financial part of the hospital. He was always well groomed, shined shoes. I still know him. He's a widower and since I lost my husband, he gives me good advice on the coping with the loss of my husband. And being focused and having something of value to do. He is an avid golfer. We talk about all the players.

ROSE BUSBY

Rose had many talents. She was a fashionable dresser and so was I. She could fix hair and makeup as a hobby. She had impeccable, elegant designer in clothing. We would go to dances, and we were in the same sorority at Tennessee State. She was reserved, spoke quietly and was calm. We loved to go out to lunch to chatter-chat.

BUDINIA KINIKACHA

We were friends, and her mother got her everything she wanted. If there was something of her own you wanted, she'd throw things out her window at night so no one else could see her do it.

One day I admired her brown loafers and a green skirt. She told me to come by after ten o'clock that night. I didn't really believe she meant it, but once I was standing beneath her window, she quietly pushed the window up and tossed the skirt and loafers out to me. I waved as I picked them up. She waved and gave me the "okay" sign.

I still can't believe she did that. And I still can't believe I kept the shoes and skirt for many years thereafter.

CHAPTER 4

POLITICS IN NASHVILLE

In college, I was a sociology major, but I always had an interest in government which I first developed in the classes taught by Mrs. Reed in high school.

On campus during the Vietnam War era, how did being in college and talking with people about the war motivate you. I wasn't too vocal about it. The demonstrations against the war were happening on all the college campuses, but I didn't go to any of the protests. I wasn't actively marching in the protests because you're supposed to be non-violent, and I didn't think I could stand them spitting at me. So, I chose not to go. It was a good decision on my part.

When students were marching and getting arrested for the harassing law enforcement, they needed a lawyer. So, I assisted Attorney Zephaniah Alexander Looby, Attorney Avon Williams and Attorney Robert E. Lillard at the time, doing legal research necessary for the defense of the students. These three lawyers had their own practices, but they worked together to defend the students who were arrested.

After college, I put my degree in Sociology to work as a counselor for the Tennessee Department of Corrections for many years. I counseled teenage girls. As they were serving their sentences in juvenile detention, I met with them in my office at the Vocational Training School. I had a caseload, and I would see each girl and we discussed things regularly. I also went to Tullahoma to deal with the girls in the system there. Driving back and forth to manage the caseload I had 50 or 60 girls to follow. I did this for several years on Hyman Street in Nashville, and I made house visits to those in foster care, but most of the girls were in the correctional facility.

I had two girls who lived in a foster home, and I saw them often when they were away from the correctional institution. They both did well. They finished high school and one of them went on to college, which I was very proud of. And we kept in contact with one another.

One of the girls I remember best was Barbara. The foster mother, Mrs. Ross, knew I was coming to visit every time I did, and every time I saw her, she appeared to enjoy helping the girls. I felt that she depended on me to help her guide the girls she fostered, and I felt I was adding positivity to all their lives.

ഇരു

The afternoon traffic seems slower than usual as I drive to the Ross's home. Finding a parking spot takes me a few minutes longer than usual, too. I begin to feel that I'm arriving late, and as I walk up the steps to the door and ring the bell, Mrs. Ross, opens the door as if she's been waiting for me. The living room is welcoming, and Barbara is sitting at one end of the couch.

"Good afternoon, Mrs. Ross," I say as she swings the door wide for me to enter.

"Good afternoon, Miss Jordan. Please make yourself comfortable."

WHAT'S UNDER THAT HAT?

"Thank you. I'm sorry to be a few minutes late. The traffic was moving slower than usual today. I hope this is no inconvenience to you."

"Oh, no, of course not. Barbara has a lot going on at school this evening. They're doing the dress rehearsal for the Fall play, and she has a speaking role."

"Yes, Miss Jordan. It's not a very big role, but I'm in almost every scene. I play the part of a nosy neighbor who meddles in everything. She's funny!" Barbara says.

"Sounds to me like you enjoy acting."

"Yes, I certainly do. I've made some friends who also like to act, and it gives me a feeling of belonging to something a little bigger than me."

"That's a wonderful thing about acting. And it's a gift if you can take on the role to become the character you play."

"I'm doing better in my math class too! And history and English are my favorites. I think I've crossed over the line into a new life, where I can see myself doing something valuable to me and to those around me when I get older."

As we talk, I see Barbara as one of the few who will move up in life and do well.

"I expect you will do just that, Barbara. Keep focused on learning everything you can. But also have fun. High School is all about discovering who you really are."

"And thanks to you, Miss Jordan," Mrs. Ross says, "I agree that Barbara is going to do just fine once she's finished with her detention and graduates from high school."

༄༅

WHAT'S UNDER THAT HAT?

Often teen-aged girls in a correctional institution find themselves in the system because their parents didn't want to deal with them. Barbara didn't commit a crime. She was from a broken home and felt abandoned by both her parents. To express her feelings, she acted out against her mother, and tried to be as difficult as possible. Sometimes, there's nowhere else for these girls to go when they're rejected by their parents, and so they end up in the foster care system or in the correctional system.

But some of the girls did commit serious offenses. When I would visit them, it was in the women's prison. Some of the girls I mentored in the prison turned out to have a decent life. But a lot of the girls who were there didn't commit a crime, and so, I know it had something to do with the parents.

Barbara had been a juvenile delinquent, but the foster mother succeeded with her. Years later, I saw Barbara as a young adult. She had graduated out of the system with a high school diploma, and so at eighteen years old she was considered emancipated by law and she was working and paying her own way.

WORKING MY PLAN

I worked as a secretary for a judge, and I transcribed the minutes of the court for quite some time. Then after that I worked for "Model Cities." An agency where they were assisting the city with different projects, such as rebuilding the decaying parts of the cities. They focused on North Nashville, and I raised hell because of that because I thought they should look at south Nashville where the black communities were located. These communities needed rehabilitating, and I raised hell to help make that happen, which it did.

I raised hell in a 'Proper" way, which caused them to take action not only for the upper-class blacks in North Nashville, but also for the poorer lower-class blacks in South Nashville. And I pointed out that they were taking care of the black communities that were already doing well, and ignoring the black communities that were struggling. I just told them right over wrong. And I knew what that meant because I grew up in the projects.

I went directly to the people responsible for deciding where to put the improvements, and they didn't want to see me coming, because they knew I'd be raising hell.

I went to Mr. Drake heading up the program for Model Cities many times. Once they started dealing with me and they realized that if things didn't go a certain way, they'd be dealing with me, and that's how I kept them accountable for sharing the improvements on the South side of Nashville as well. And I enjoyed that.

※

"Here we go again, the same old same old, because you know I'm here for a purpose, Mr. Drake. You're doing so much for the people in North Nashville, and forgetting about these people in South Nashville, And you know that's NOT right. Model Cities is supposed to represent all of the people in North and South Nashville. And I, as a member of the Metro City Council, represent South Nashville. And that's why I'm here. I don't have to tell you what to do. You can look at the community and see what needs to be done. And that's what you get paid for!"

Lois and Mr. Drake both knew that if he wasn't responsive to her questions, she would go above him to get people higher up to influence him.

Mr. Drake spoke up quickly, "Okay, okay, okay! We're going to improve the broken sidewalks and add additional sidewalks where they're needed."

"Well, I know exactly where we need them. Why don't we go together a take look."

"All right. Let's see. Today's is Wednesday. Could we go Friday?"

"I'll meet you there at 11 o'clock Friday morning. At 4th Avenue and Chestnut."

First elected in 1974, Jordan speaks now as a political strategist. She is a political tactician since that race for the District 17 seat she won by campaigning door to door.

∞⚭

The day is warm and sunny as Lois Jordan drives her convertible, top down, along the streets of the white part of the 17th District on the other side of the tracks from where she lives. Her district is divided by railroad tracks, literally and symbolically defining the divided culture of the current day. After a while, she parks her car and takes her dog, a German Shepherd named Banner, from the back seat and retraces her journey on foot. Her plan is to walk past every house and business on that side of the tracks to make herself visible and to normalize her presence in the community. If anyone speaks to her, or even seemed interested in speaking with her, she introduces herself to them and then after some conversation, asks for their votes.

As her voyage progresses, she comes to a house where a white man is sitting on his front porch next to a spittoon, which he uses as Lois Jordan tries to gain his vote.

"Good afternoon, Sir, my name is Lois Jordan and I'm running for councilwoman on the Metro Council."

WHAT'S UNDER THAT HAT?

He pauses for a moment and then says to her, "I don't vote for Niggers."

"Well, we have something in common—I don't either," she says. "I'd like to know what you think that word means. The word nigger."

The man sits for a moment, spits in his spittoon, and looks Lois in the eye.

"I'm not sure. It's just word people say."

Lois could hear the ice breaking around him.

"Well, let's just agree it's not a polite word. It's best not to use it. But, Sir, I'm also wondering what it is you do for a living. And how the issues of the 17th District affect your life."

As they talk, he expounds on his viewpoint concerning the issues. And then, he reveals that he is a business owner.

"You know, young lady, I like you. And I like your ideas. And, in particular, I want you to know that because of my business located here in the 17th District, I hear a lot of opinions from my customers about the way things are going. I know everybody, and I am sure I could be very helpful to you in your campaign."

"I would be very pleased to have your support. If you'd like, you could become the team leader for this side of District 17. And I'd be happy to attend any events you can put together to provide me a chance to talk with your customers."

"I'd like that very much," the man says.

"Let's set a time to meet at your business, this week if possible, and start a plan."

"All right. Tomorrow at eleven in the morning. Would that work?"

"Yes Sir, it certainly would!"

And with his help Lois Jordan won the election, becoming the first elected women council member and also the first black woman council member ever elected to the Metro City Council.

☙❧

STANDING UP FOR HERSELF IN THE COUNCIL MEETING

As Lois begins her four-year tenure as a councilwoman on the Metro City Council, the first thing she realizes is that the Council is made up of thirty-nine men and one woman—herself, Lois Jordan. Those wishing to speak to the Council begin to fill the seats lined up before the council. They come to talk to the council. At first, that she is the only woman in the chamber makes Lois a little weak in the knees.

Several times during the meeting, Lois raises her hand to speak, but no one recognizes her. Well into the meeting, she realizes that if she doesn't make a point of speaking, she won't get a chance to participate at all in any meetings that follow.

Fed up, Lois takes a sip from the glass of water standing next to the microphone. Then she stands up. She bangs her hand on the desk over and over again until she has their attention.

"Councilmen, most people normally refer to me as Lady Jordan because I always wear pearls and dress with style. Right now, there's a lady standing on the floor. I have listened to you during this meeting—my first as a council member—and you should listen to me. I came prepared to contribute to this council meeting, but, when I have tried to speak you don't recognize me to let me speak."

After a short silence, the Chairman of the council says, "Gentlemen, clearly, we need to allow Lady Jordan to participate in our meetings. She has the courage of her convictions, which allows her to call attention to our rudeness. And on behalf of this council, I apologize to you, Lady Jordan, for our impolite behavior. From now on, you shall be referred to as Lady Jordan, and we shall include you in our conversation."

SECOND YEAR ON THE CITY COUNCIL

I was against busing—a very important issue in the 1960s and 1970s—so, as a City Councilwoman, I went to school with the kids to see what they were dealing with.

※※

Tennessee weather is warm as the schools open again each year. This year the sky is dark, and a misty rain falls as Lois Jordan arrives at Glencliff High School. Early arrivals begin before dawn. Buses carrying students to Glencliff for their first day of school pull up near the entrance. As the students leave the buses, Lois Jordan sees that the children carry no umbrellas to protect them from the rain. So, they take shelter under the overhang high above the entrance that affords a narrow strip of dry pavement where they are able to stay relatively dry.

"Good morning, everyone. My name is Lois Jordan, and I'm on the Metro Council. Looks like we have a rainy day for the first day of school this year." The students nod but say nothing. "I'm just wondering how early you had to get up to be here at 6:25 a.m."

One girl raises her hand. "I got up at 4:30 this morning to catch the bus by 5:15 It's a long ride to get here."

WHAT'S UNDER THAT HAT?

Another girl raises her hand. "We have to come this early so the buses can drop us off and then go do their regular routes to transport the local students."

A boy speaks up. "Yeah, the doors to the school open at 7 a.m., so we have to wait more than half an hour outside, no matter what the weather is."

Another boy joins in the conversation. "I'm already so tired, I only hope I can keep my eyes open during the day."

Lois nods as she listens to their comments. "Let's wait here together for the doors to open."

☙☕

I learned by talking with parents of bussed children just how inconvenient it was for the parents to participate with the children in the schools where they were bussed for the simple fact that it wasn't easy to get there. And often the children had to wait as long as two hours before the buses picked them up.

The 'powers that be' wanted busing, in spite of the fatigue it caused in the children and the difficulties it caused for the parents. Busing was the beginning of breaking down the family structure, and I wanted to stop that if at all possible.

The bus system wasn't ready to meet the load of students who were encouraged to go to school far from their homes became understandably upset because the children and parents of the communities had to wait for buses that came hours late or not at all. The newspapers reported the situation as follows:

"I received a telephone call from one of my constituents at about 9:30am telling me that kids had been waiting for about an hour or an

WHAT'S UNDER THAT HAT?

hour and a half for a school bus at Claiborne and Cannon."

When Miss Jordan went to the scene and found 70 or more children at one school bus stop and about 100 more at another stop down the street.

"When bus 191 came by it was loaded. After I called, and later sent a parent to call — the line stayed busy for about half an hour — eventually a bus did come about half loaded and picked up a few kids," Council woman Jordan said. "It picked up 25 or 30 of the children. The rest of them went home. The parents are complaining because apparently not enough school buses are coming into this area. I am personally encouraging parents to send their children to school."

In the afternoons, Lois went knocking on doors and asked parents to send their children if they hadn't already.

ஐஇ

Lois walks up to the bus stop where Mrs. Lawrence, mother of five children, had called her to come see the situation. The crowd of worried parents surrounds Lois.

"Mrs. Lawrence, explain to me what's going on."

"Oh, Dr. Jordan, we've been waiting here for the bus since 8:15 this morning. That's the time we were supposed to be here. The bus came just after 10 a.m.

Mrs. Wright joins in. "Yesterday the bus didn't come until ten o'clock and today my two children waited and it was ten o'clock again before the bus came."

Mrs. Martin chimes in. "The same thing happened for my two children. These buses are coming too late for the children to attend school for the whole day."

Mrs. Lawrence speaks up again. "And what about the bus for

going home? What time will it arrive here so we can walk our children back home? It costs us $4.80 to get the child to school and back when a child misses the bus. If the bus doesn't come on time, what are we to do?"

Mrs. Wright adds, "That's a lot of money for us to pay whenever a child misses the bus that doesn't come on time, and no one does anything to make sure the buses run on a clear schedule. We have to pay for the school district's mismanagement of the buses. And it's not fair at all."

Mrs. Martin says, "And a lot of us parents have missed a full day of work, too. We want our children to ride the bus. It's a new experience for them. It needs to be regular and predictable."

Mrs. Lawrence adds, "And then there's the question of where they will stand in bad weather—when it's raining and snowing. There is no shelter where they catch the bus."

Lois feels the frustration of her constituents. "I'll do everything I can to make this situation right. There is no excuse for the buses to be so late. A few minutes, perhaps, but hours on end? That's not all right."

The mothers thank Lois for her efforts and then turn to go home.

༄༅༄

I wanted to be true to my word. I was puzzled as to why so few senior Cameron students from the 17th District I represented on the Metro Council rode on bus 297 to the new McGavock Comprehensive High School in Donelson. It was one thing to see the problem, it's another to experience the problem. I knew there should be many more students on the bus because I personally canvased the

WHAT'S UNDER THAT HAT?

area and received assurances from parents that their children would go to school.

So, I arranged to have a *Nashville BANNER* reporter and photographer with me to follow bus 297 on its fifty-mile-long route one morning at the start of the school year. Why did the bus pick up only six students at the Second Avenue and Hart Street stop? And why were there no other Cameron students at the four other Cameron area pickup stations?

The Supervisor of school-community relations and other school officials said they were surprised to learn of this issue. Supervisor Carothers said, "The rain had stopped by 7:50 a.m. when bus 297 started its pickup run. We are assuming that some students drove to McGavock. A number of students assigned to bus 297 got on other buses going to McGavock. Some parents called us asking directions to McGavock and so, we are assuming they drove their children to school. And then, there are students who have summer work and will not report for school at McGavock until the following week."

I didn't think that "tensions" played any part in the Cameron seniors failing to show for the first ride to the new school, the largest and most modern school in the South. I had talked with many parents and students on the phone on Monday, advising calm. I believe sound-thinking parents realize that since the laws of our land have spoken, they are going to send their children to school on buses. They want them to have an education, black and white.

❧☙

All-in-all the issue of bussing students to schools far from their homes each day played out all across the American educational system. Some were willing to participate, and other were not enthusias-

WHAT'S UNDER THAT HAT?

tic about it. But to listen to the responses of the students bussing to Donelson their perspectives were mixed.

The first student on bus 297, Susie Weiland, age sixteen, said, "I'm happy to be going back to Glencliff to finish my senior year." Her mother, Margaret Weiland said, "I agree with my daughter's happiness." They lived directly across from the first pickup station on Glenrose Avenue.

Mrs. Little took a contrasting point of view to her daughter, Janice, an eighth grader who boarded bus 297 at Pillow and Martin streets for the long ride to Donelson Junior High School. "I don't like it," said Mrs. Little. "I got another one being bussed to Murrell Elementary, and I don't like that either. We just moved to Nashville from Ashland City, and we are liable to move back." And when asked to estimate the mileage from the pickup station to Donelson Junior High, she replied, "Ye gads! From here to Donelson? I don't know how far that is."

One of the six black students picked up at Second Avenue and Hart Street, Richard, age twelve, said, "It's all right, but..." as his voice trailed off into silence.

Mary, age fourteen and an eighth-grade junior high student taking the bus to Donelson, said, "It's really all right, but I wish it wasn't so far."

Mary's sister, Pam, age twelve, a seventh grader going to Donelson as well said, "I didn't think the ride would be especially fun. I get car sick."

Eventually, the scheduling was corrected, and bussing continues to serve the children in out-lying areas and in places where the local schools have closed.

WHAT'S UNDER THAT HAT?

⛬

YEARS THREE & FOUR ON THE CITY COUNCIL

Lois Jordan's interests included Social Services, such as funding food stamp programs, finding housing for the homeless, and providing a non-official social worker to help them find shelter. Council reps could work with the churches to coordinate between the city programs and the church programs. To accomplish her goals, Lois Jordan started an on-going dialogue for the betterment of the communities.

From 1974-1978 while Lois was on the Nashville Metro City Council, she was also a member of the National League of Cities. And because she was a minority member, it helped others to join the National League of Cities.

The National League of Cities (NLC) is an organization comprised of city, town and village leaders that are focused on improving the quality of life for their current and future constituents.

With nearly 100 years of dedication to the strength and advancement of local governments, NLC has gained the trust and support of more than 2,700 cities across the nation. Our mission is to relentlessly advocate for, and protect the interests of, cities, towns and villages by influencing federal policy, strengthening local leadership and driving innovative solutions.

At NLC, we are committed to a culture that values diversity and promotes inclusion and belonging. We are focused on building more inclusive communities and improving the quality of life for current and future residents. We strive to build teams at NLC that mirror our members and the communities they serve. Equity is a guiding principle for our work. In our mission to relentlessly advocate for and protect the interests of cities, towns, and villages, we believe in a fair distribution of resources based on a community's needs and a just approach that recognizes the impact of historic disinvestments in marginalized and underrepresented communities.

☙❧

Lois Jordan is a multi-faceted person whose many professional experiences supported her endeavors during her working years. Often times, these life experiences over lapped.

She was a bank officer at a local Nashville bank. This helped her get to know many people, including businesspeople, who had their accounts in the bank. And she also was a Real Estate agent for over forty years, buying and selling properties, rehabbing properties and selling them.

She served many charitable organizations, working with them to fund-raise for those citizens who needed their services.

All of these areas of interest wove together into the beautiful tapestry of Lady Jordan's impact on the communities she served in Nashville before, during and after her time on the Metro City Council.

BANKER

I represented the Commerce Union Bank as a liaison in the community where my major responsibility was to produce profitable new time, demand and trust customers for the bank.

I initiated methods of securing new business. Also I maintained and created relationships with present and prospective customers.

WHAT'S UNDER THAT HAT?

These deposits were obtained by contacting and soliciting new and additional business from healthcare institutions, consumer organizations, governmental agencies, educational institutions, business agencies, charitable and civic organizations. I made a list of prospects and made systematic calls to administrative staff of these various institutions.

Also, I developed and initiated seminars in the bank and local communities by going to these institutions and giving seminars.

SEMINARS

I brought people together in a meeting room in the bank for meetings starting at seven o;clock in the evening. Of course, there was an overhead projector showing information for the seminar. We sat around a conference table and enjoyed refreshments: such as coffee, water, and juice with cookies as a snack.

These people were very happy to be invited to a bank and treated with professionalism. They included presidents of companies and universities, as well as leaders in the Tennessee Government. It was my job to successfully encourage them open accounts with the Commerce Union Bank.

I invited the large corporations to come to the bank for our seminar about our customized banking services for charities like the Red Cross who would receive specialized tracking of funds raised for tornado relief, for flood relief, wildfires, and other kinds of disasters.

Commerce Union Bank also offered checkout counter donation containers in local businesses, sponsored fundraising events with donors, holiday donation bell ringers of the Salvation Army, and mail-in campaigns.

WHAT'S UNDER THAT HAT?

ଇଓ

CHARITABLE ORGANIZATIONS

Lois Jordan worked actively for many years for charitable causes and organizations spanning four decades with her service. Here are just some of her accomplishments.

2016
The American Cancer Society: Lois was involved in developing the Nashville Gala to celebrate the organization's fundraising success.

2002
The Nashville Symphony Guild: Lois Jordan served as Chairman of the Directory

1998 and 1999,
American Red Cross: Lois Jordan sat on n the Board of Directors, and served on the Patrons Committee for the Initial Rhapsody in Red benefit. Also, she served on the Research and Public Relations Committee.

1996 and 1998
The Nashville Chamber of Commerce: Lois Jordan served on Education Task Force Committee and the Government Relations Committee.

WHAT'S UNDER THAT HAT?

1994

The State of Tennessee. The honorable Mary Pruitt for the 58th District recognizes Lois Jordan by this office and presents *"The Unsung Heroine Award"* on the 8th day of June 1994 to Lois Jordan in recognition of "her dedication to patient service given to educate the children the State of Tennessee to prepare them for full participation in society and the generous time she gave in guidance extended to our future leaders."

1976

March of Dimes: Lois received a Certificate of Appreciation for helping the National Foundation of the March of Dimes reach its goals for the prevention of birth defects and disability effort and support of the Salk Institute for Biological Studies.

1974

Friends of Children's Hospital at Vanderbilt: Lois Jordan served as the District Chairman.

Lois Jordan also sat on the Boards of the Susan G. Komen Breast Cancer Foundation and the Nashville Ballet Board, Nashville Opera,

CHAPTER 5

HEALTH, SURVIVAL & WISDOM

Dr. Lois Jordan's example teaches us all how to contribute in meaningful ways to our communities. As a young woman, raised in the projects of Nashville, Tennessee, Lois rose above her circumstances to become the first Black-American female elected member of the Nashville Metro City Council.

Her determination to learn, to grow and to meet all the right people pushed her forward and upward and away from her humble beginnings. But Lois is only human, and as she entered the seventh decade of her life, she faced a private enemy she never thought she'd have to fight—a small lump in her left breast.

❧☙

"See that little shape right there?" The doctor points at a shadow on the X-ray. "Probably a just cyst," he says to comfort his patient. "These things are fairly common. But we'll need to biopsy the lump to find out for certain what it is. It's not a difficult procedure. I'll use this syringe to pull some of the material from the lump. It's almost painless. All right?"

WHAT'S UNDER THAT HAT?

Lois looks at the doctor and nods.

As she leaves the clinic, Lois feels confident the lump will be something benign.

"I don't have time to be sick right now. I'm sure it's like he said, a cyst."

But the churning in her stomach signals it might be something more.

☙❧

The phone rings incessantly as Lois goes to pick it up.

"Hello? May I ask who's calling?"

"Hello, is this Dr. Lois Jordan?"

"It is…"

"Dr. Jordan I'm the nurse at the Cancer Center. We have your biopsy results."

"Oh?"

"Dr. Jordan, I'm calling to let you know you have breast cancer."

The moment it takes to process this information grows long as Lois's surprise turns to anger.

"You're calling me to tell me something like that on the phone?"

The silence feels like an eternity to Lois. She hangs up the phone with more force than she expects and without another word. Then she sits down on a chair in the kitchen to think. The anger rushes at her like a river swollen from a storm. She tries to contain her rage but lets out a shriek that rattles the windows. The release is followed by a torrent of tears. Then a calm settles upon Lois's mind and brings her into the light of reason.

"Breast cancer, huh? I have to see my doctor."

WHAT'S UNDER THAT HAT?

☙❧

The waiting room fills with people of all persuasions as Lois waits for someone to call her name. Lois doesn't read any magazines. She doesn't watch the television that is showing a morning game show. She sits unmoving, thinking about the situation this cancer will cause for her. Then, through the fog of her thoughts she hears her name.

"Lois Jordan, please follow me."

She stands and walks a few steps behind the young woman leading her to an examining room to meet with her doctor. As she allows the girl to take her temperature and measure her blood pressure, Lois doesn't speak.

"Please wait here. The doctor will be in shortly. You don't need to change clothes for this consultation," she says quietly, and then leaves Lois alone in the room.

It'll be fine. That nurse made a mistake calling me. It's really nothing.

A short rap on the door breaks the silence, and Lois startles. The door opens. Her doctor smiles as he pulls the rolling stool over to talk with her.

"Hi, Lois. It's good to see you," he says as the wheels rattle him into position. "I'm sorry the nurse's call was so impersonal. I think we need to re-think that part of our process."

"Yes, that would be good," Lois says, searching the doctor's face for some hint of her situation.

"Well, the good news is that the cancer hasn't spread to the lymph nodes. So, a round of chemo and radiation treatments should kill the tumor, and we'll remove the breast to make sure there's not chance for a recurrence."

WHAT'S UNDER THAT HAT?

"Sounds difficult to me," Lois says softly. Tears fill her eyes.

"It's not exactly a walk in the park, but it's a very effective means to the desired end—no cancer."

The doctor's matter-of-fact description of the coming treatments leads Lois into a new mindset. Endure the prescribed regimen, knowing the effects it will have on her body in the short term, while looking forward to the promise of a cancer-free future.

"I guess there's no way around this. And I take solace in the fact that this cancer hasn't spread. That's a blessing."

"That it is," the doctor says, allowing a smile to flow across his face. "You're a strong person, and this little lump isn't going to stop you."

୨୦୧୧

Lois turns her situation into a means to communicate with a broader audience by speaking at health groups in the region, including the Susan G. Komen organization. She joins the Board of Vanderbilt's Children's Hospital, which gives her other opportunities to share her perspectives on surviving cancer and the motivation it brings to turn a bad situation into a good one. But years following, in 2021, Lois experiences another setback so many older people fear.

୨୦୧୧

Lois wakes in the night, dry-mouthed and thirsty. Harold is snoring softly next to her.

I'll get some cold water in the kitchen and put in some ice to melt away this dryness.

Her bare feet touch the rug next to her side of the bed, and as she walks toward the hallway, the cold hardwood floor sends a shivering chill up her legs. The streetlights beyond one small window offer only a weak glow, and as she feels her way to the stairs, the shadows fill in the dim view ahead of her.

She puts her right foot out to take a step down and misses the second step altogether. She feels her lost balance pushing her forward, and then the hard edges of the uncarpeted wood steps punching her side and beating on her back. She hits the floor hard. A sharp pain accompanies the snap of a vertebrae in her neck as she falls limp as a rag doll on the foyer floor.

She lies there, for an eternity it seems.

Harold wakes with a start from the commotion in the hallway. He gets up and makes his way toward the stairs. He looks down to see a dark figure on the floor below. He holds the banister as he steps onto each step.

"Lois? Lois! Can you hear me?" No answer. Harold panics as he takes the phone from the foyer table and dials 911.

Lois hears the conversation.

"911, what's your emergency?"

"My wife fell down the stairs, and it seems she's unable to get up. Please come. She must go to the hospital."

"Your address, Sir?"

As Harold gives the address, Lois relaxes, knowing she will be in good hands when the paramedics come.

℘ℭ

Cat scans, MRIs, and the reality that the fall broke her neck makes Lois upset and testy.

"Lois, you need to wear this collar without fail for five months. If you don't, your neck will not heal," the doctor says. "It's uncomfortable but equally unavoidable. Wear it you must!" as he secures the brace around her neck.

"I hate this! How am going to wear my fancy hats? Five months with this thing on my neck? That's not a medical treatment, it's a prison sentence!" Lois opines as she sits rigid and crabby to her core.

Harold takes her home in the car and helps her into the house. They sit at the kitchen table while he gets the lunch he made in the early morning and lays the meal out on the table.

"Lois, I made this casserole to cheer you up. Please take a few bites."

"I can't. I can't look down. I can't lift the fork and knife. I'm not sure I can even chew the food. And this awful collar is hot and itchy! It makes me miserable in every way."

Harold manages a weak grin. "Well, then, I'll feed you until you can feed yourself."

He takes a bite of the casserole onto her fork and offers it to her. She opens her mouth. She chews slowly. She smiles.

"It's delicious, dear. Thank you." He kisses her cheek.

"I love you, Lois."

"And I love you." She points at the fork. And he feeds her again.

೫೦೦೪

For five months Harold waits on Lois hand and foot, helping her do everything we all take for granted. She complains, and Harold makes her smile every time.

Then one day toward the end of the five months, Lois stops Harold as he's walking near her.

"Harold, come sit with me a moment."

He sits next to her on the couch.

WHAT'S UNDER THAT HAT?

"Harold, I've known all along that I was going to get well. You know I believe in Destiny, don't you?"

"You've said so many times."

"I've kept the faith that I would heal completely, because I know I still have so much more to do in this life."

"Yes, you do, darling. Yes, you do."

❧☙

LADY JORDAN'S WISDOM FROM LIFE

If you don't control your attitude, then your attitude will control you.

If you don't like my words, don't listen. If you don't like my appearance, don't look. If you don't like my actions, turn your head.

Accept your past with no regrets. Handle your present with confidence. Face your future without fear.

Confidence is like a building. Don't let others knock you down. Use the bricks they throw to build yourself up.

What hurts you today makes you stronger tomorrow.

Life is too short. Laugh when you can, apologize when you should, and let go of the thing you cannot change.

Don't tell people your dreams, show them.

WHAT'S UNDER THAT HAT?

Most people want to see you do better, but not better than them.

When someone gives you their trust, they are saying, "I am safe with you." Don't break it, appreciate it.

I was told to always forgive how bad people treat you. But it is damn hard to forget. Instead, treat them right, because in life what comes around goes around.

Everybody makes mistakes. You don't want to be judged by anyone else at the end of the day. The past is unchangeable, but people change, and life goes on.

There is no limit to what we, as women, can accomplish.

Grace, strength, intelligence, fearlessness, and the nerve to never take no for an answer.

I raise my voice, not so I can shout, but so that those without a voice can be heard. We cannot succeed when half of us are held back.

If you don't see a clear path for what you want, sometimes you have to make it yourself.

Whenever women gather together failure is impossible.

My mother told me to be a lady, and for her, that meant be your own person, be independent.

CHAPTER 6

GET AN EDUCATION

MY YEARS AS A TEACHER IN THE METRO NASHVILLE PUBLIC SCHOOLS

Even while I was growing up in the Napier homes—even as people around me were ending up dead, pregnant or in jail—I always knew that I wanted to attend college. I always intuitively understood that education was the key to your freedom. And that without it, there weren't too many appealing roads that you could follow.

Bad times don't discriminate. And I knew that there was always a chance that life wouldn't go my way. But I knew that, at the very least, if I didn't get an education, I'd be back in bad times for certain.

Beyond the classroom, my education helped me develop other skills. An education isn't just about academics. I had always loved singing, pantomiming, dancing and acting, so I joined the glee club and the dance club at Cameron. Extra-curricular activities helped me develop confidence and blow off steam outside the classroom, helping me relax before I tackled my school assignments.

I loved school so much in fact, that I became an educator. Before joining the city council, I worked at correctional facilities for girls throughout Tennessee and as a probation counselor in a juvenile court. For many years I also worked as a teacher at Pearl Cohn, Maplewood High School, and at Ewing Park Middle School in the

WHAT'S UNDER THAT HAT?

Metro Nashville Public Schools system. I taught government and economics in a very similar position to my mentor, Mrs. Reed. Because of her, my teaching philosophy involved lots of hands-on work, with plenty of field trips and projects. I had my students writing to dignitaries, to the mayor, to the governor, to the local representatives.

I invited my students to attend sessions at the city council chambers to watch legislators give presentations and debate bills, among many other activities where they met people they would not have met any other way.

Educating is a tricky thing. The teacher must take the student from the textbook and apply the textbook to real life. That's when students really begin to understand how things work.

Throughout my time as a teacher, I had several opportunities to move into the MNPS central office. I might have made more money, but I would've had to sacrifice being in the classroom. Ultimately, that was a trade I wasn't willing to make. Halfway through my career, I decided to go back to school and earn my doctorate in education so that I could earn a larger salary while working as a classroom teacher.

At this point, I've been out of the teaching field for many, many years. Still, I sometimes run into my former students at church or around town in Nashville or Hendersonville. They're always happy to see me, and I'm always happy to see them.

"Man you were tough!" they often remark. "Tough, tough, tough. I never worked as hard as I did in your class."

"Well," I always respond, "now that you've had some time to think about it, don't you think that toughness was good for you?" Where would you be today if I hadn't been tough on you?"

"Well, I don't know," they'd usually say. "Certainly not where I am today!"

One of my favorite students—whom I mentored—is named

WHAT'S UNDER THAT HAT?

Ms. Jolanda Pender. She was a focused student. She was always eager to pick my brain. She was a leader. She didn't know everything, but she was always willing to scratch and claw and fight until she found the answers that she sought. She was a great asset to me as a teacher because of her leadership. She would always do her work and set the example in the class. She had a relationship with the other students who wanted to be like her. When they saw her working, they got to work themselves. She's doing very well for herself at present. She's both a mother and a former tax accountant.

I also have fond memories of mentoring Mr. Victor Wynn. He is a Nashville native who earned a joint law and divinity degree from Vanderbilt University. Recently, he's found a passion at Temple Church in Nashville, where he worships, serves as a pastor, and directs the choir. He was the first African-American to ever serve as student council president at Hume Fogg Academic Magnet High School, likely the best public school in Tennessee.

I also mentored Susan Tucker, who is now a lawyer, and DeCosta Hastings, who is now a city councilman. I also worked with Reverend Omar Lee, who is a minister in a local church.

Victor, Susan, DeCosta, Omar and Jolanda weren't born with silver spoons in their mouths and didn't have all the advantages, but they made their circumstances work for them. There a many great teachers in American public schools. You are not bound by your circumstances. Go to class. Question everything. Think outside the box. Earning an education can help you transcend any circumstances of your upbringing or that cross your path in life and maximize your potential.

WHAT'S UNDER THAT HAT?

THE GREAT EQUALIZER

Many different sources can lead you astray in today's world. Today's news media are extremely negative and can be disruptive to the youth. There's a very conservative media and a very liberal media. Each side is polarized and constantly taking shots at each other. It makes it nearly impossible to know what the truth is. For different reasons, both sides enjoy targeting our current school system. This negativity can make today's youth think, *Why even bother with school?*

I watch both conservative and liberal news programs so that I can see what both sides are saying, and then I make up my mind about who is right or wrong. I would strongly encourage today's young people to do the same. An education involves learning constantly outside of the classroom. An education involves more than just schooling. Learning to hear different opinions, think critically about them, and make up your own mind is a crucial skill. The sooner that you can develop it, the better.

For my money, the best way to consume the news is by reading. Television programs are glossy and flashy with their productions, but hard news is best consumed in newspaper form. Make it a part of your routine to inform yourself about what ever is going on in the world on each particular day. That way, you can talk to all sorts of people about all sorts of topics.

Young people from broken homes may also see their peers skipping school. Perhaps their friends are selling drugs and moving up in a local drug organization. Perhaps those people seem more like role models because they seem to have money and status, definitely more that people their age who are in school. This is a mirage, a fallacy. This is short-term thinking. An education is more stable, solid and—in the long term—profitable than any drug or crime-centric life could possibly be.

I saw plenty of people take this short view in the Napier and Sudekum homes. These people were willing to grab a quick paycheck by turning to crime, completely disregarding their education and their own potential. While it may be difficult, youths from troubled areas need to look past these early temptations for long-term gains. And for the sake of their own integrity and honesty, they need to be willing to work for something better.

Getting involved in extracurricular activities—something like sports, music, and debate—can also help today's youth feel more of a pull toward their school and their education. Band, glee club, and student council gave me a sense of belonging that would have made me enjoy going to school every day even if I didn't like my classes (which I did).

According to Abraham Lincoln's Maslow's Hierarchy of Needs, belonging is the first thing that we need after our basic physiological and safety-related needs are met. Clubs, organizations, and teams at school provide today's youth with a place to belong and a place to connect with like-minded peers.

Just like I faced a fork in the road early in my life and made the choice to surround myself with people who would take me higher. Today's youths can give the easy choice—the criminal life—the cold shoulder and opt to really participate at school. Students who really lean in at school are ofter the happiest, the best-adjusted, and the most successful later in life. Even those who come from broken homes in the projects.

WHAT'S UNDER YOUR HAT?

A BLUEPRINT FOR YOUR SUCCESS

PART ONE

MAKE YOUR PLAN

The previous chapters in this book outline the way my life unfolded and introduced some of the people who mentored me, some of the events that shaped me from childhood and throughout my entire life. Maybe you could see yourself in some parts of my story.

But you are you. And your life is unique to you. I am talking with YOU in this section of my book. I will offer you ideas and options to consider to get you started.

Perhaps you are just starting to become who you will be.

Perhaps you are in high school and trying to decide what's the right next step for you.

Maybe you're a young adult who jumped into working at minimum wage jobs right out of high school, and now you realize you need something more to satisfy your heart and your mind.

Perhaps you dropped out of high school and feel like you're floating on the wind without a clear passion, dream or view of what you want your life to look like.

Maybe you're still living with your parents.

WHAT'S UNDER THAT HAT?

Or maybe you're homeless, without any idea how to save yourself from the streets.

Well, if you can read, you can do anything you truly want to do and learn all the skills you'll need to become a successful, self-reliant, person who contributes in a positive way to the lives of others and to society.

That sounds like a big mountain to climb, doesn't it?

It's actually just a matter of breaking the huge goal into many smaller steps. Some steps will take more time to accomplish. Other steps will seem easy and you will accomplish them in short order. But, most of all there are essentials that you need to move forward from where you are to arrive at the destination your life is meant to reach.

MAKE YOUR PLAN

- **To make a plan you must accept that you are not limited to your current circumstances. You have it in YOU to make the changes that you need and want to make.**
- **To make a plan, you must surround yourself with mentors who know what you need to learn and who want to impart their knowledge to you. They are all around you.**
- **To make a plan, you must get the eduction that provides you with the skills you need to fulfill your plan. This doesn't always mean going to college.**

Think about what you already know about yourself. Only YOU know what you like to do and what you don't like to do. These things show up early in life. Think about yourself as a child or young person. What did you like to do best?

Maybe you liked to fix and build things. Go to a Trade School.

WHAT'S UNDER THAT HAT?

Maybe you liked to dress up and make your own clothes. Go to a Fashion Design School.

Maybe you liked to cook and wanted to be a chef. Go to Cooking School.

Maybe you liked to draw, paint, model clay or make art out of unusual objects. Go to Art School.

Maybe you liked to play with makeup and design hairdos. Go to Cosmetology School.

Maybe you liked working with computers. Go to Computer Technical School.

Maybe you loved to sing and make up songs. Go to Music School.

Maybe you liked fixing bicycles and cars. Go to a School for Mechanics.

Maybe you liked that little lemonade stand you set up as a kid. Or you shoveled the walks for others in the winter. Or your raked leaves, or did babysitting, or helped an elderly couple keep their house clean, or one of thousands of other small jobs that help others. So, maybe you're an entrepreneur—a person who is good at selling something that others want to buy, or providing a service that other people need.

POSSIBILITIES ARE ENDLESS. TURN THEM INTO YOUR REALITY.

Become essential to others with the skills you gain and you will always have a job—a job of your own design.

I can hear you now. Is this you?

"But, Lady Jordan, I don't have any money. I can't afford to go to school."

WHAT'S UNDER THAT HAT?

My answer to you is, "You can't afford NOT to go to school."

There are many non-profit organizations that make the learning part of a job as an intern or as an entry-level employee. This means "school" isn't limited to the public and private schools in this country. These are places where you can get started in learning the skills you need to MAKE YOUR PLAN work. And you can earn money while working your plan. You may discover there are several things you become interested in learning about and that variety of skill and knowledge can lead you to a very busy and successful life.

A simple Google Search is all it takes to start your journey.

Don't tell me you don't have a computer. Do you have a smart phone? That's all you need. No smartphone? Go to a public library. They have computers you can use for free.

YOUR PLAN IS ENTIRELY UP TO YOU–AND ONLY YOU!

DRESS THE PART

Because of Mrs. Galloway, I never looked like I was a little girl from the projects. I always wore a suit for professional activities. When you see a lady in a suit, you sit up and take notice. I always wore pearls, gloves and a hat. I had a signature look. Always proper, always professional. That helped me achieve things in politics, despite the disadvantage I had being a woman, being young and being African-American.

I never left my house without looking like the First Lady. Nothing made me feel more powerful than leaving my house and heading

WHAT'S UNDER THAT HAT?

downtown wearing my white suite and my white hat. I often brought my dog and usually had money in my pocket. I remember turning heads and grabbing people's attention. When people looked at me, they would assume that I was a woman who was very well to do, a woman who knew where she was going.

Dressed in my 'uniform,' I felt the courage to talk to anyone. A lot of times, people are shy when they don't need to be. Whenever I left the house, I would know exactly what I looked like without even having to look in the mirror. I knew where I was going. I knew I was strong, and I knew that I could leave all of my hangups at home. This confidence was a key element in really believing that I could carry out the plan I'd always had for myself.

I realize that confidence comes more naturally to some people than to others. My advice to those who struggle with confidence is to practice.

- **The first step is realizing that everyone has something worthwhile to offer.**
- **Practice telling yourself who you are and what contributions you can make.**
- **If you think you can't make any contributions, you definitely won't make any contributions.**

Don't let anybody turn you around. Strong people are not turned around. You keep on moving forward. And while it may seem like a small thing, the right clothes and the right self-presentation can help you out with that.

ଛ୨ଙ

WHAT'S UNDER THAT HAT?

SAVE SOME MONEY FOR YOURSELF

I never like the idea of folks begging. I saw plenty of it in the projects, plenty of people who had fallen on hard times. When I was growing up in the Napier Homes, I swore that I would never have to beg. My mother's reaction to the welfare worker likely played a big role in shaping my attitude in that regard. I didn't want to fall victim to that situation.

Early on, I learned that each dollar I got was actually worth 75 cents. I gained this knowledge by surrounding myself with people who took me higher. They taught me that I couldn't get something for nothing. If I wanted something, I had to prepare for it and work for it. I decided to prepare by being very, very, frugal.

I saved a quarter from every dollar. I put the change from any cash purchase into my piggy bank or in my savings. Slowly, through these two practices, I accumulated a nest egg that insulated me against unemployment, poverty, and other financial hardships.

YOU CAN DO THE SAME

75% of your income goes to expenses.
25% or more of your income goes to savings.

The Acorns app can perform these functions for you. It rounds up your purchases to the next dollar and invests that spare change in index funds. You can also schedule recurring investments from your bank account, allowing you to treat each dollar as if it is actually worth 75 cents.

Once you accumulate some savings, I believe that real estate is an excellent safe house for your money. Throughout my life, I've bought several properties, fixed them up, and either rented them out or flipped them. I saved up money for a down payment on my first house. Then I let that house buy another house. And I let that house buy another house. And I let that third house buy another house, and so on. I ended up with twenty pieces of property.

You generally can't go wrong when you buy real estate because the value of your property is usually going to increase. Throughout history, the real estate market has always trended upwards. And I'm a firm believer in history repeating itself.

WHEN YOU HAVE ENOUGH MONEY GET A GOOD FINANCIAL ADVISOR

You may think you can freelance, but when it comes to your money—and your life—it makes sense to have a professional holding the reins.

I ended up getting really caught up in the recession. During my teaching years, I remember following all the doom and gloom on television about the stock and real estate markets. But, my financial advisor helped me through it, and I emerged from it stronger than ever.

NOTHING IN LIFE IS FREE.

SOMEBODY IS ALWAYS PAYING FOR IT. PREPARE YOURSELF.

Now it's your moment to start making your plan. Here are some guidelines and questions to use as you begin Your Plan.

WHAT'S UNDER THAT HAT?

Get a ruled pad of paper or a spiral bound notebook to write your answers.

THESE ARE THE FOUNDATION OF YOUR PLAN.

1. Describe my life five years from now. (Be bold and imagine the best life for yourself.)
2. Describe my life ten years from now.
3. What are my current circumstances?
4. How can I change those circumstances to fit My Plan. (Maybe you need to get a temporary job to earn some money and a Piggy bank or money box to save that 25%.)
5. What areas of interest appeal to me most when I imagine a career? (It's all right to have several areas of interest, but line them up with the most interesting career ideas first.)
6. Who are the people in my life *right now* who can help me get going in the right direction? (Teachers, Ministers, Business Owners you already know.)
7. When will I talk with these people to ask them to help me, to be my mentors. Write down dates to contact each person, and get their contact information. Go to see them or call them and set up a meeting.
8. What intern programs or entry-level employee jobs can I get in my area(s) of interest? (List at least two for each area of interest).

9. How will I get information about these programs.

10. When will I follow through by contacting these programs.

11. When I look in the mirror, what do I see?

12. How do I need to dress to appear more professional?

13. I will need a savings account in a bank to save 25% of my income. Select a bank near you for this purpose.

14. When I have $100 saved up, then open my savings account. What is the date I'd like to reach this goal?

15. When do I want to start my first internship or entry-level employee program?

Now you have the first beginnings of Your Plan. It's time to put it in motion. Follow up with all these opportunities you've selected and see what works best for you.

WHAT'S UNDER YOUR HAT?

A BLUEPRINT FOR YOUR SUCCESS

PART TWO

HOW TO GET THINGS DONE

"A good woman knows her past, understands her present, and moves toward the future. A good woman does not live in fear of the future because of her past. Instead, she understands that her life experiences are merely lessons."
—I Thinks This Applies to You, *Catherine Young-Broussard*

Ultimately, a lot of working your plan comes down to having a strong belief in yourself. Along the way, there are going to be bumps. There are going to be obstacles. Bad times don't discriminate.

But, greatness is measured by the obstacles you've overcome and the people whose lives you have touched, not by the amount of money you've made. So, if you encounter challenging obstacles, you actually have a better chance at greatness.

Throughout it all, you must remain organized. During your journey, there are going to be some rocky mountains and some tall peaks. But if you have a plan, you can summit these mountains and bag these peaks. Those who summit Everest spend years planning and succeed thanks to the efforts of mentors (and sherpas).

WORK YOU PLAN.
WORK YOUR PLAN.
WORK YOUR PLAN.

You've got to work your plan, doing whatever it takes to get there. Outline clear goals early in the process and know exactly where you want to go.

I learned how to put my plan into action in large part by reading a single book: *The Technique of Getting Things Done,* by Donald A. Laird. I will share a couple of key insights that can help you get things done yourself.

BE A LIFELONG LEARNER

One of the best ways to make money during the first 30 years of life is to invest it in reading what counts. Saved money may be lost, but hoarded knowledge sticks and multiplies at an illegal rate of interest." — **Chapter 5**

༺༻

Throughout history, countless innovators, thinkers, and dignitaries have been inspired by reading books. The best choice you can make is to be a lifelong learner. In biological terms, if you aren't growing, you're dying. As such, never stop learning, and never be too arrogant to think that someone might be able to teach you something.

WHAT'S UNDER THAT HAT?

Reading omnivorously—newspapers, magazines, fiction, nonfiction, biographies, anything really—can help you come up with your next idea, or just inspire you to char a certain course of action. Never stop reading and never stop learning.

☙❧

"Human efficiency rises and falls. Bodily processes have both high and low points during the course of the day. Mental powers wax and wane as the hours progress. This 'diurnal course of efficiency,' as it is called, can be used to get more things done. The daily rise and fall of mental efficiency follows a course like this for most persons.

MORNING

8 o'clock: 105 percent

10 o'clock: 102 percent

AFTERNOON

1 o'clock: 101 percent

4 o'clock: 96 percent

EVENING:

8 o'clock: 98 percent

10 o'clock: 97 percent

— Chapter 13

WHAT'S UNDER THAT HAT?

ଚ୍ଚର

Throughout history, many different people have figured out how to harness this "diurnal course of efficiency," Surgeons often follow a schedule that mirrors the table, as they need their minds to be as clear as possible to perform their high stakes work.

A Chinese proverb highlights that — *If you lose an hour at the start of the day, you'll spend the rest of the day working for it.*

ଚ୍ଚର

Slaves have to work, whether they like it or not. So do many free men, as far as that goes. Their pocketbooks are in their jobs, their hearts are elsewhere. Most of the world's Doers spell money in small letters, WORK in capitals. Getting things done is their main objective. — Chapter 13

ଚ୍ଚର

If you only work for money, you'll burn out quickly. You'll spend frivolously in order to combat the boredom and lack of meaning you feel at your job, trying to replace meaning with things.

Instead of seeking things—and by extension, money—seek knowledge and meaning. It is foolish to assume that money means nothing. But a frugal person can live on many different salaries. If your work is more meaningful, and if you feel as though you are constantly growing during your job, you will earn more money because you will feel more inclined to stick with your job.

WHAT'S UNDER THAT HAT?

Figure out exactly what you bring to the table—along with what you enjoy and find meaningful—and use that to map out your plan, both for your career and for your life.

SPEAK UP

I've emphasized time and again that no one is going to hand you anything in life. Nothing is free, and anything that seems free likely has strings attached or was paid for by someone else. And if you want something in life, you need to take action. You need to first voice that you want it. Then you need to make a plan to get it and then you must execute that plan.

There is nothing shameful about voicing your desires. Many people expect youths, especially girls, to stay quiet, to be seen and not heard. When I was young myself, I did not subscribe to that theory or conform to those expectations. I told everyone that I was going to make it out of the projects one day and make something of myself. And ultimately, I was able to do that, in part because I spoke it into existence.

I also pride myself on my ability to listen. I like to listen to people in conversations and let them feel as though they are steering the proceedings. I believe this quality allows me to talk to and connect with a wide range of people, including those with far different backgrounds than my own.

Nevertheless, there is a time to use your voice. For me, that moment was running for city council. I felt like I could make a legitimate difference in the lives of my constituents, and that I was the best person for the job. I voiced that, and ultimately I got the result I wanted.

You can't get what you want unless you acknowledge—both to yourself and to others—exactly what it is you want to accomplish.

WHAT'S UNDER THAT HAT?

Get your notebook so you can do the following exercise:

IT'S NEVER TOO LATE TO BECOME WHO YOU ARE SUPPOSED TO BE?

In Chapter Six your determined the beginnings of your plan. Now it is time to add fuel to drive your plan forward.

1. List your dreams and passions—they fuel your goals and give you the persistence to survive the inevitable pitfalls and bumps in the road of your journey.

2. Which dream is most important for you to accomplish? (If you have several dreams you want to accomplish, list them all in order of importance.)

3. Explain why do you think you will be able to realize these dreams.

4. Explain what accomplishing your dreams will do for you and help you accomplish Your Plan.

5. List five people you are going to talk with about Your Plan. This is how you give voice of Your Plan to others and you may find more mentors willing to help you.

6. How did you feel while talking with each of the people you listed.

7. Were you able to clearly explain Your Plan? Why or why not.

8. What suggestions did these people give you? Explain which of these suggestions you want to use and why.

9. Do these suggestions truly fit you and your plan? If so, explain why. If not, explain why.
10. List the knowledge you still need to gain for Your Plan.
11. How will you gain this knowledge? There are infinite training lessons on www.YouTube.com for every kind of skill you can imagine. Many are free to use.
12. Also www.amazon.com has all kinds "How-to" books in every category you can imagine. These books offer invaluable experiential knowledge and training resources.
13. Re-write any part of Your Plan than has changed because you are now gaining more knowledge and more mentors.
14. Now condense Your Plan into one or two sentences.

As an example, here's my plan in two sentences:

I want to run for city council because I believe I can make a legitimate difference in the lives of my constituents in District 17. I am confident that I am the best person for the job because I grew up there and my education and experiences in life bring me to this moment ready to serve the people who need the most help.

൸൪

The two sentences you write and then memorize will tell anyone you meet what you are planning to do. These two sentences become your "Elevator Speech"—something you can share in thirty seconds or less with anyone, anywhere, and anytime.

Now write your two sentences into this book and then be sure to memorize them.

WHAT'S UNDER THAT HAT?

MY VOICE AND MY PLAN:
DATE: ___ /___ /_____

_____
_____
_____
_____
_____
_____
_____
_____

Now, go speak up about your plan.
You will be surprised what happens.

WHAT'S UNDER YOUR HAT?
A BLUEPRINT FOR YOUR SUCCESS
PART THREE
FAITH IS EVERYTHING

"We must develop and maintain the capacity to forgive. He who is devoid of the power to forgive is devoid of the power to love. There is some good in the worst of us and some evil in the best of us. When we discover this, we are less prone to hate our enemies." —*Martin Luther King. Jr.*

"Determine to grow your faith. You do that through the spiritual disciplines of prayer, Bible study, sharing your faith, gathering with other believers for worship and the living out of your faith. And, never waste a loss, you must learn from them."
—*Dr. Bruce Chesser, Reverend, First Baptist Church of Hendersonville, TN.*

"Sometimes it hurt, but it didn't hurt me."
—*Reverend Lester E. Stratton of Rockland Baptist Church in Hendersonville, TN.*

"Live in community with other believers. The Christian life is not lived exclusively between God and the individual. It is lived in community with other believers."
—*Hebrews 10:23-25*

WHAT'S UNDER THAT HAT?

GOD'S CHILD

When I was a child, I attended the Holy Family Catholic School in Nashville. Every day, I would walk from the housing projects to the Catholic school, which was off Lafayette Street, and back again.

Throughout my life, I've maintained my involvement in various churches around Nashville. Currently, I sing in the renowned choir at the First Baptist Church of Hendersonville, led by Greg Crane. Singing in the choir has provided the glue in my faith, so to speak. I sing out my love of God, and I get to worship in the company of a group of like-minded people whom I admire, respect, and care for dearly.

My faith has made me more patient and brought more joy into my life. Knowing that the Lord went through so many things for us has made be realize that I can accept and deal with any hardships I come across in my personal life. Given the teaching of the Lord, I've been more willing to sacrifice for others, including my husband and my students.

When I wakeup every morning, I pray that my day will go a certain way, and this and that and the other. But I don't expect to get everything that I wish for: I believe that He may not come when you really want Him to come, but He is always there. He'll come unexpectedly. But you have to stay in the faith, really stick with it.

Going to church has strengthened me and ingrained these beliefs in me. At First Baptist, I look forward to seeing the people and the people look forward to seeing me. To me, that's what community is all about. Although I came from a Catholic background early in my life, First Baptist has really grounded and uplifted me.

WHAT'S UNDER THAT HAT?

The reverend Bruce Chesser has the God-given talent of being able to relate the reaching of the Bible in an accessible and everyday manner.

Reverend Chesser and the men and women at First Baptist have affected me in ways beyond my comprehension. Alongside them, faith has become an even stronger pillar of my everyday life. When I pray every morning, I feel grateful to have such a supportive, Christ-centered community.

THE IMPORTANCE OF FAITH

I believe faith offers innumerable benefits to today's youth. At times, it's difficult to reach the youth. They don't want to buy into faith. It's difficult to get them involved. Often, they don't come to church on their own. They have to be encouraged. Faith isn't an act where you walk alone. You have to walk with somebody. I believe that the youth know that there is a higher being, but they need to be encouraged. The best place for that is a "Connect Group" where they an receive individual mentoring.

I believe that every single person—especially young people—should be open to joining a faith-based community. Not only can individual mentorship at Connect Group change your life, but the lessons and teaching you learn from the Bible can help you figure out the plan that you want to work for the rest of your life.

It's never too late to give yourself to God and start going to church. I've found First Baptist Church to be a particularly welcoming community, but I know that tons of churches around the world provide homes for all sorts of people. A church community can give you direction, a purpose, a reason to get up out of bed in the morning.

If you're feeling your life is without direction, walking through those church doors and sitting down in one of those pews is a great place to start. Finding something bigger than yourself can put any trivial problems in your life that seem important issues into perspective.

ꜱꜱ☙

My mother's decision to go to work and decline welfare made a strong impression on me. It instilled in me an independent streak upon which I pride myself to this day—an independent streak that has been paramount to any success I've had throughout my life.

That lesson was key for the rest of my life: If you want something, you've got to work for it.

When I was growing up in the Napier homes, I had my first love. Even with all of my grandiose plans and ideas, I was human like anyone else. I wasn't a stiff young lady. I had a little bit of the devil in me. We all have some of that. He was a tall drink of water, a good-looking man. He hailed from a very affluent family. In fact, his mother and father came to my wedding years later. I love them. They were considered some of the elite in the community.

At some point, I found out that he had been messing around with other women on the side. And he'd managed to get one of these side women pregnant. He didn't want to get married to her. He wanted to marry me. He came to me, crying and groveling and sniveling. He knew he was supposed to get married to the mother of his unborn child, but he wanted to run away.

On the day of his wedding, I made sure that he went to church and got married. I forced him to march down the aisle at the church. All three of us—the young man, the pregnant woman, and I—all belonged to the same church, so this pregnancy was quite a storyline. He wasn't all bad, as he ended up loving that baby very much. So did I.

That incident with my lover only entrenched me firmer in my

plans, my beliefs, and my desire to escape my circumstances. An unwanted pregnancy and being trapped in a relationship was exactly what I didn't want, and because that incident took place so close to home only served to spell it out for me more clearly.

I moved out and got my own place when I was eighteen. I was ready to start the next phase of my life, and I really didn't want to live in the projects anymore. While I appreciated what the projects had taught me, I was ready to see what life beyond the chain link fence held in store for me.

YOU ARE THE MASTER OF YOUR FATE

"Greatness is not measured by what a man or woman accomplishes, but by the opposition he or she has overcome to reach their goals."
—*Dorothy Height*

"With every experience, you alone are painting your own canvas, thought by thought, choice by choice."
—*Oprah Winfrey*

"It's not about how much money you make. It's about the difference you make in people's lives." —*Michelle Obama*

As Ms. Height emphasizes, tougher circumstances provide you with a larger capacity for greatness. The more you overcome, the more greatness you achieve. If you start out in a tough situation—in the projects, with a single mother, without anything to eat but sugar and bread—there's a silver lining: you can achieve more greatness than those who started with more.

WHAT'S UNDER THAT HAT?

Of course, that greatness won't achieve itself. I hope that my story demonstrates that you don't have to live in the ivory tower, with carpets on the floor, eating gourmet dinners every night, with both parents living together, in order to be successful in life. But you do need to accept one of the universe's fundamental truths:

Only you are the master of your fate, and you have a great deal of control over what happens to you.

If you accept Him, God certainly plays a huge role and can show you the correct path. But, even with God on your side, you need to be the one taking action and making things happen.

During my years as a teacher, I saw many youths who were born into difficult circumstances. The one who transcended those circumstances demonstrated grit, work ethic, tenacity, and integrity. While qualities such as intelligence may not be in your control, you can fully control how gritty, hard working, tenacious and honest you are. You have the power to control what you can control. Often enough, what you can control is enough to get you to where you want to be in life.

☙❧

PHOTOS

Dr. Lois Jordan honored in New York City by P. O. W. E. R.

*Lois Jordan with two Marine escorts
at the 2019 SAINT NICHOLAS Charity Ball*

Lois Jordan talks with other honorees at the 2019 SAINT NICHOLAS Charity Ball

Lois Jordan (on the right) with the other honorees attending at the 2019 SAINT NICHOLAS Charity Ball.

Dr. Lois Jordan stands with a microphone in the Metro Council Chamber as she relives the moment that contributed to her moniker, Lady Jordan. (Photo by Clint Confehr)

*Lois Jordan Honored
at the 2019 SAINT NICHOLAS Charity Ball*

Cardell Jordan (Lois Jordan's younger brother) and his wife Sandra at a formal event when they were younger and living in St. Louis.

STUDENTS THANK DR. JORDAN

Thank you, Dr. Jordan,
We are so blessed to have you as a teacher. Thank you for caring like no one else did. Thank you for taking the time and effort to help us and support us. Thank you for having high expectations. Thank you for challenging us. Thank you for believing in us. May your life be as joyous as you made ours!

Sally Bebawy

Dr. Jordan:
Yer like da grrrreatest!
~~Eric Lee~~
DAVID SHIN

Well I tell you what dang ole Cheesenips & chicken wing ~~Wah~~ Wahwee! Sean

Your 900 hail hate-
chase

Dr. Jordan,
You are a nice teacher. This was my first time in summer school and I really enjoyed it. I will never 4-get you.
-Christy Baldy

LOVE, LORENA

Thanks for giving me the edge I need to make it in the real world
-Amy you

HOW CAN WE POSSIBLY THANK YOU ENOUGH?

greg

You've given me so much more than you will ever realize. God knew I needed something and sent you to give it to me. [?] and have

Thank you Dr. J For being the best and for pushing us to [?]

Dr. J,
You're the best teacher!
♡ [signature]

ors!

THANKS
Q

It has been a great learning experience for me. Ramesh

Dr. Jordan,
Thank you for spending your time on us!
Emily

STUDENTS THANK DR. JORDAN

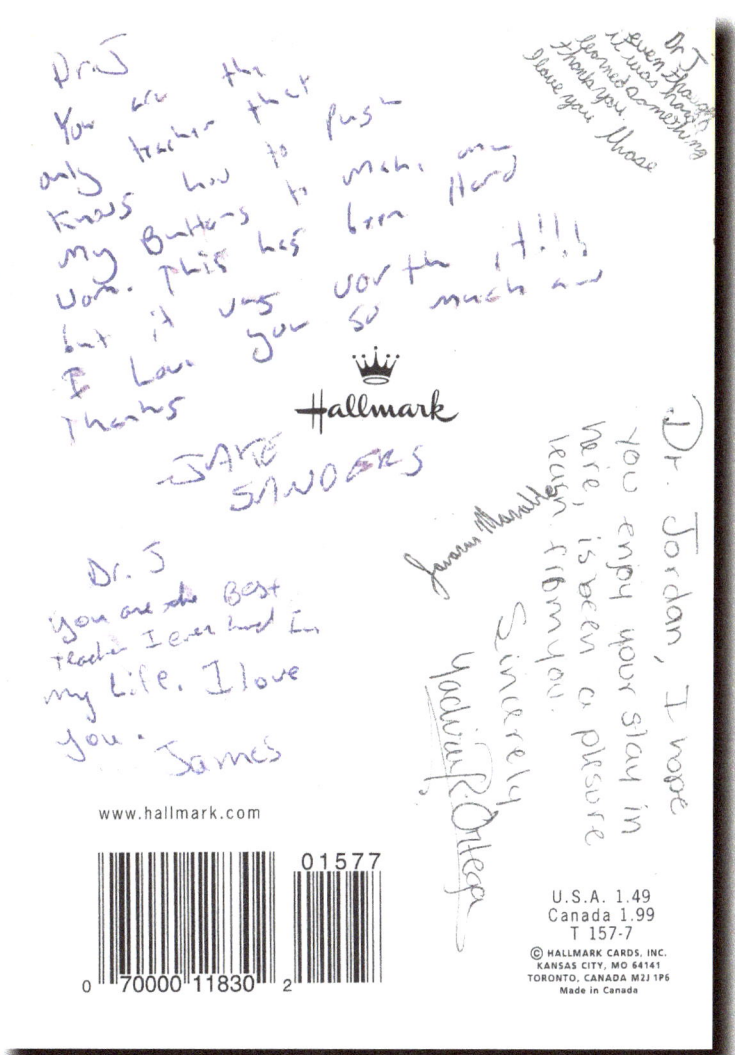

METRO CITY COUNCIL

Lois Jordan was inducted as a Colonel Aide de Camp on the Governor's Staff when she was elected to the Metro City Council in 1974.

1974 METRO CITY COUNCIL

24 New Faces on Council

1974 METRO CITY COUNCIL

★★★★↑★★★★
LOIS JORDAN

Mentors & Dignitaries

MENTORS

Two of the most influential people in Lois Jordan's young life were Robert Emmitt Lillard and Mrs. Galloway. He taught her the ropes of politics, and she taught her make a great first impression.

Robert Emmitt Lillard
Lois Jordan's Primary Mentor before, during, and after her service on the Nashville Metro City Council.

Mrs. Galloway gave Lois the confidence to dress the part to show others where I was headed. And I learned from her how to make a lasting impression on just about everybody I met.

DIGNITARIES

Lois Jordan (2nd from left) with Ladybird Johnson (front right) at an event in the mid-1970s.

Mrs. Jordan, thank you for your support and friendship as a Charter Member from Tennessee. With your help we can make America stronger, safer and more prosperous.

Best Wishes,
Laura Bush   George Bush

Governor, Phil Bredesen
Governor of Tennessee from 2003-2011

*Dr. Lois Jordan with Governor Mike Huckabee,
Governor of Arkansas from 1996 to 2007.*

ABOUT THE AUTHOR
DR. LOIS JORDAN

AUTHOR
DR. LOIS JORDAN

Dr. Lois Jordan comes from humble beginnings in Nashville's housing projects. She lived with her mother and sisters in a two-story town home in the J. C. Napier Projects, which stood among the worst—and all that term implies—for how urban, low-income housing projects were conceived to be.

When Lois moved into her Grandmother's house as a teenager, her life began to change. She realized the simple truth that—if she was going to escape poverty and a hard life in the projects—she would need to earn a good education. Elizabeth Reed, her Civics teacher in high school, saw Lois's potential and guided her with constancy and imagination so Lois could pursue her interests in history and government. And, pursue them she did.

Lois became a teacher and taught government studies and followed in Mrs. Reed's footsteps with her hands-on teaching style.

Through her time on the Metro City Council, Lois remained engaged with the schools and dealt with many of the educational issues of the day, including school busing.

Later in life she was involved in philanthropic organizations, and she continued to be involved in the political issues of the day.

Today, Dr. Lois Jordan lives in Hendersonville, TN, and is still making a contribution to community life there.

This book is her memoir and represents her continued effort to guide young people toward a better life with her clear-eyed advice on how to succeed through education and mindful application of that education in their own lives.

www.ingramcontent.com/pod-product-compliance
Lightning Source LLC
Chambersburg PA
CBHW042138160426
43200CB00020B/2978